MW00399367

Nature Watch Austin

Nature Watch Austin

GUIDE TO THE SEASONS IN AN URBAN WILDLAND

Lynne Weber and Jim Weber

Text and Illustrations by Lynne Weber

Photography by Jim Weber

TEXAS A&M UNIVERSITY PRESS • College Station

This paper meets the requirements of ANSI/NISO Z39.48-1992
(Permanence of Paper).
Binding materials have been chosen for durability.

Library of Congress Cataloging-in-Publication Data

Weber, Lynne, 1961–
   Nature watch Austin : guide to the seasons in an urban wildland / Lynne Weber
and Jim Weber ; illustrations by Lynne Weber ; photography by Jim Weber.—1st ed.
      p. cm.
   Includes bibliographical references and index.
   ISBN 978-1-60344-431-6 (book/pb-flexibound : alk. paper)—
   ISBN 978-1-60344-481-1 (ebook format)
   1. Natural history—Texas—Austin.   2. Natural history—Texas—Edwards
Plateau.   3. Wildlife watching—Texas—Austin.   4. Wildlife watching—Texas—
Edwards Plateau.   5. Seasons—Texas—Austin.   6. Seasons—Texas—Edwards
Plateau.   I. Weber, Jim, 1955–   II. Title.
   QH105.T4W43   2011
   508.764'31—dc22
   2011010694

To Our Parents,

Who encouraged an

unbounded exploration

of the wild things and wild places

of our childhoods

Contents

Preface

"In every walk with nature,
one receives far more than he seeks."

JOHN MUIR

THE purpose of this book is to provide the reader with a month-to-month guide to the natural events that define the seasons in the City of Austin and surrounding areas. While not a true field guide, trail guide, or location guide, it is perhaps best described as an interpretive nature handbook of native wildlife and wild places. Nature is full of interesting stories, unique patterns, and curious facts. As such, this book is intended to appeal to all lovers of the outdoors, from birders to butterfliers, gardeners to hikers, and conservationists to wildflower enthusiasts.

For weeks at a time, each season allows us to experience the natural cycles in our environment. As naturalists, we look forward to the return of the flora and fauna that every season brings. Trees bud, birds migrate, wildflowers bloom, frogs chirp, and butterflies flutter by. Through increased awareness and careful observation we can have a general idea when we might expect to experience these wonders and look for them with the anticipation created by each change of the seasons.

We hope readers will use this book as a way of introduction to some of the natural wonders of the Austin region on the eastern edge of the area known as the Edwards Plateau. Each chapter will feature a few profiles of flora and fauna that are particularly interesting or noticeable at that time of year, with some suggestions on how and where to see them. The reader will also be presented with some seasonal data as well as photographs and sketches of the subjects and/or concepts. For the purposes of further study, the appendix will include lists of area field guides, parks and preserves, and other in-depth sources of information. While a huge diversity of species exists in this region of Texas, we cannot cover every topic and have chosen to focus on those that are likely to fascinate most nature-watchers.

Each species will be referred to using common names, but when first introduced, scientific names will also be included. While common names are more easily remembered by beginning naturalists, many common names can exist for the same species, so providing the scientific names can serve as a way to eliminate any confusion and provide a basis for continued study. Scientific names rely on the binomial classification system, where each species name is in Latin and has two parts. The first is the genus, literally meaning descent, family, type, or gender, and the second is the species, which is a general term for the specific name or descriptor of that species. When a specific species can only be identified under a microscope or through DNA analysis, its genus name is given followed by "sp." to represent a group of closely related species. Scientific names are usually typeset in italics, with the genus name always written with an initial capital letter. Occasionally, a third part is included and is denoted as a distinctly occurring sub-species or variation.

Predicting the exact timing of events in nature can be tricky business, and may depend on several variables such as rainfall amounts, temperature changes, food abundance, and hours of daylight, to name a few. We highlight events as they might occur under normal conditions, but encountering the unexpected is one of the joys of observing nature. Any errors or omissions are truly our own, and we'd appreciate hearing about something we may have missed. Send suggestions to us at naturewatch@austin.rr.com.

Acknowledgments

E ven a labor of love requires the ongoing support and encouragement of a team of many like-minded individuals. While we derived much pleasure from the work itself, our gratitude goes to the entire staff at Texas A&M University Press, but especially to Shannon Davies whose immediate kinship and keen expertise made possible the finished product you are holding in your hands. Her confidence in our ideas and our trust in her guidance were constant companions.

There are many to thank for their assistance with subject research, content review, photography, and field work. Experienced observers, nature enthusiasts, and professional scientists alike have all contributed their time and energy, including John and Kendra Abbott, Bill Carr, Dee Ann Chamberlain, John Chenoweth, Willie Conrad, Alison Cook, Andrea DeLong-Amaya, Samantha Elkinton, Renee Fields, Paul Fushille, Clark Hancock, Kirsti Harms, Aaron Hicks, Wendy James, Alfred and Linda Kilian, Joe Lapp, Greg Lasley, Marsha May, Kathy McCormick, Dave Mollendorf, Roger Myers, Jack Neff, Kelly Nesvacil, Jim and Lisa O'Donnell, Julia Osgood, Theresa Pella, Frances Pfertner, Mike Quinn, Jennifer Reidy, Bill Reiner, Scott Rowin, Margaret Russell, Mark Sanders, Steve Schwartzman, Kathy Shay, Cappy Smith, Jason and Lisa Spangler, Kevin Thuesen, Kunda Lee Wicce, and Russell Womack.

Most of all, we owe a huge debt of gratitude to Roland (Ro) Wauer, who took us under his wing shortly after we arrived in Texas over twenty years ago, and re-forged our conscious connection to the natural world. Thank you, Ro, for being such an inspiring mentor, and for reminding us that with discovery comes knowledge and with knowledge comes responsibility. We hope this book serves as a portal into the wonders of nature in Austin, reminding us all that we are a part of nature and not apart from it.

The hills of northwest Austin with Pennybacker Bridge in the distance.

Introduction
to the Ecology of the Edwards Plateau

L ocated in Central Texas, the Edwards Plateau is a "physiographic region," meaning it has distinct characteristics in terms of landscape, plants, and animals. The eastern edge of the Edwards Plateau is very abrupt and forms a steep escarpment, a feature actually visible from space. A true plateau with a relatively flat topography, the Edwards Plateau is situated at a higher elevation than regions to the southeast. On its southern and eastern edges, however, many rivers have eroded downward and cut steep valleys into the plateau, creating the canyons and adjacent hills. The erosion by these rivers creates the landscape that we call the Texas Hill Country.

The rocks underlying the Edwards Plateau are layers of limestone that were deposited in a warm, shallow sea during the Cretaceous Period about 100 million years ago. At that time, the area of the Edwards Plateau was located closer to the equator, and the climate of the Earth was generally warmer than today's climate. Limestone formed as a chemical precipitate from the water in this warm, shallow sea, along with the deposited calcareous remains of billions of tiny sea creatures. During the drainage of that ancient sea and the formation of the Gulf of Mexico, a break and a slip occurred in the Earth's crust, centered along a linear fault zone. Running in an arc from west of Uvalde to about Waco, this fault zone forms the primary recharge zone of the Edwards Aquifer, where water runs off the higher elevation areas west of the fault and drains into the lower elevation areas east of the fault. Before the building of reservoirs along our river systems, the Edwards Aquifer was once one of the only sources of drinking water for our region.

Time, wind, and water erosion have revealed many of the limestone layers. Of those layers that are currently exposed, the youngest layer is called the Edwards Formation. Once hundreds of feet thick, most of this layer has been eroded away and only about 50 feet or less remains on the tops of the highest hills. This limestone is characterized by its numerous sharp holes, and is often the "Swiss cheese" rocks we trip on when hiking the upper ridges. The next oldest layer underneath the Edwards is a transition zone called the Walnut Formation, which developed when this area was near the shore of an adjacent landmass. It contains abundant fossils of many types of shallow-water marine creatures, and includes silts and sands washed off of the land. As you might expect, this layer is soft and crumbly (often called "marl"), and in it you can find several marine fossils, mud crack impressions, and even dinosaur tracks.

Beneath the Walnut, and often the oldest layer we can see easily, is the Glen Rose Formation. It represents the vast majority of rocks exposed at the surface of the plateau. The rocks of the Glen Rose are much more varied, created by deposits from salt marshes, beaches, lagoons, deep sea water, and flowing river water, which means that during this period there were many shifts between land and marine-based environments. Because of this variation, hard and soft rock alternate, and as the softer rock erodes more rapidly, large bands of the harder limestone are exposed. This gives the hills their terraced or balconied appearance, and hence the Spanish name balcones.

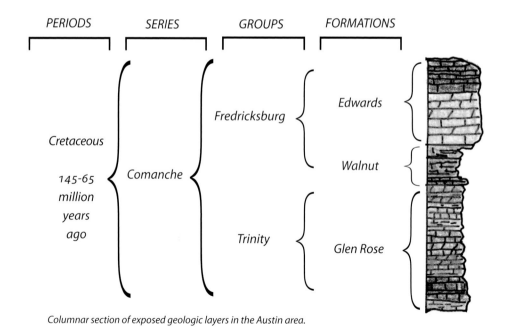

Columnar section of exposed geologic layers in the Austin area.

Introduction

Edwards limestone is a hard, often sharply pocked layer of rock able to transport water to the aquifer.

Because of the unique geology and resulting soils formed from the limestone deposits, Central Texas is a very biodiverse area with a large number of different species of plants and animals. In 1992, voters in the City of Austin passed Proposition 10, approving $22 million in bonds for the sole purpose of acquiring and improving lands to protect water quality, conserve endangered species, and provide open space for passive public use. Jointly owned and managed by the City of Austin, Travis County, Lower Colorado River Authority, The Nature Conservancy of Texas, Travis Audubon Society, and various private landowners, these lands, collectively called the Balcones Canyonlands Preserve (BCP) System, are planned to grow from the roughly 28,000 acres set aside today to over 30,000 acres by 2016.

The BCP is actually a system of preserves consisting of several tracts of land in western Travis County. A well-loved jewel within this system is the Bull Creek Nature Preserve (BCNP), 1,140 contiguous acres located primarily between the eastern border of Jester Estates subdivision and Loop 360. The BCNP is an example of prime habitat for the endangered Golden-cheeked

The erosion of alternating layers of hard and soft limestone form the Balcones.

Warbler, a bird species that is found to breed only within Central Texas' specialized mix of mature Ashe Junipers (locally called 'cedars') and stands of live, Spanish, and shin oak trees. This type of mixed oak-juniper woodland grows mainly on moist steep-sided canyons and slopes, providing the warbler with the food, water, and nest-building materials it needs to breed.

In addition to the Golden-cheeked Warbler, seven other endangered species make the preserve system their home, including the Black-capped Vireo, Tooth Cave Ground Beetle, Tooth Cave Pseudoscorpion, Tooth Cave Spider, Kretschmarr Cave Mold Beetle, Bone Cave Harvestman, and Bee Creek Cave Harvestman. These last six species are called "karst" invertebrates, insects which spend their entire existence underground in karst formations. These formations, such as caves, sinkholes, cracks, and crevices, were formed by the dissolution of calcium carbonate in limestone bedrock by mildly acidic groundwater. Over seventy other rare plant and animal species also exist on the preserves, making this region one of the most biologically diverse areas of the country. As a result, Central Texas is happily home to more habitat conservation plans than any other region in the United States.

In 1998, the citizens of Austin also sought to protect Barton Springs, an artesian spring in the heart of the city with both environmental and historical significance, and voted to approve a municipal bond that protected the source of the springs. Now known as the Water Quality Protection Lands (WQPL) program, it employs cutting-edge strategies for land conservation and management to further its mission to "produce the optimum level of clean, high quality water from project lands to recharge the Barton Springs segment of the Edwards Aquifer." WQPL lands are made up of outright purchased tracts as well as purchased development rights or conservation easements on private property, and much like the BCP properties, are managed by staff from the Austin Water Utility and private landowners as appropriate. Many of these properties are located in the southern parts of the city, and occur in both the recharge and contributing zones of the Barton Springs segment of the Edwards Aquifer.

Activities on the land above these zones can have a significant impact on the amount and quality of water making its way to the aquifer, so managing the surface community of plants and soils is a key factor in optimizing the absorption, filtering, and release of rainfall. Encouraging thriving grasslands, building good soils, controlling erosion, limiting encroachment of trees and shrubs, and

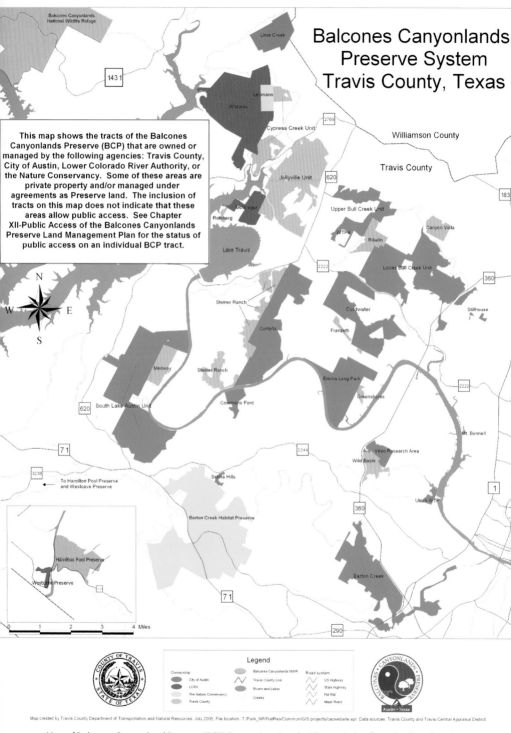

Balcones Canyonlands Preserve System
Travis County, Texas

Balcones Canyonlands
National Wildlife Refuge

Lime Creek

143 1

Lehmann

Wholess

Cypress Creek Unit

2769

Williamson County

Travis County

Jollyville Unit   620

183

McGregor

Upper Bull Creek Unit

Romberg

Canyon Vista

WTP4

Ribelin

Lake Travis

2222

Lower Bull Creek Unit

360

Steiner Ranch

Coldwater

Stillhouse

Cortaña

Franzetti

Medway

Steiner Ranch

Emma Long Park

2222

Greenshores

620   South Lake Austin Unit

Commons Ford

Mt. Bonnell

71

2244

Vireo Research Area

Wild Basin

3238

To Hamilton Pool Preserve
and Westcave Preserve

Senna Hills

1

Ulrich WTP

360

Barton Creek Habitat Preserve

Hamilton Pool Preserve

Barton Creek

Westcave Preserve

71

0   1   2   3   4 Miles

290

This map shows the tracts of the Balcones
Canyonlands Preserve (BCP) that are owned or
managed by the following agencies: Travis County,
City of Austin, Lower Colorado River Authority, or
the Nature Conservancy. Some of these areas are
private property and/or managed under
agreements as Preserve land. The inclusion of
tracts on this map does not indicate that these
areas allow public access. See Chapter
XII-Public Access of the Balcones Canyonlands
Preserve Land Management Plan for the status of
public access on an individual BCP tract.

N
W   E
S

Legend

Ownership
- City of Austin
- LCRA
- The Nature Conservancy
- Travis County

- Balcones Canyonlands NWR
- Travis County Line
- Rivers and Lakes
- Creeks

Road system
- US Highway
- State Highway
- FM RM
- Major Road

Map created by Travis County Department of Transportation and Natural Resources July 2005, File location: T:/Park_NR/NatRes/Common/GIS projects/cacwebsite apr Data sources: Travis County and Travis Central Appraisal District

Map of Balcones Canyonland Preserve (BCP) System (reprinted with permission from the City of Austin Wildland Conservation Division).

A bit of prairie along Austin's eastern edge.

keeping caves and other karst features free from debris are important elements in managing these special lands.

For 20 to 30 miles east of the Balcones fault zone and primarily east of IH-35, lies a narrow strip of Blackland Prairie, land characterized by clay-rich soils and softer limestones that support the growth of several species of native grasses and wildflowers. The deep, black soils are some of the richest and most naturally fertile in the world, but only a few remnants of the true prairie ecosystem exist today, as most have fallen to plowing, overgrazing, and urban sprawl.

All of the wild and beautiful areas in and around urban Austin require management plans in order for them to remain pristine habitats. This includes establishment of secure boundaries and rules for access control, maintenance of appropriate trails, species monitoring, habitat enhancement, and—last but not least—public education and outreach to promote good neighbor relations. As residents living near these preserves, we can do our part to become stewards of these unique habitats. While in the preserve system, we can stay on marked trails, travel only on foot, and "take only photographs, leave only footprints." In surrounding neighborhoods, we can landscape with native plants, remove

Introduction

invasive plants, eliminate pesticide use, be responsible pet owners by handling pet waste appropriately, and practice water conservation.

Most importantly, we can all minimize further negative impacts on the fragile habitat that surrounds our neighborhoods by caring for the preserves, parks, and other open spaces through volunteering. Activities you can become involved with in the preserve system include long-term habitat restoration, gathering and planting native seeds, removing nonnative invasive plants, and learning about and sharing your knowledge of the native plants and animals that make this such an enchanting place to live.

Nature Watch Austin

A misty morning dawns on Lady Bird Lake.

CLIMATIC DATA FOR THE MONTH OF JANUARY IN AUSTIN.

	January 1	*January 7*	*January 14*	*January 21*	*January 28*
Record High	85°F	80°F	79°F	82°F	79°F
Average High	60°F	60°F	60°F	60°F	61°F
Average Low	40°F	40°F	40°F	40°F	41°F
Record Low	17°F	13°F	17°F	17°F	18°F
Sunrise	7:28 a.m.	7:28 a.m.	7:28 a.m.	7:27 a.m.	7:24 a.m.
Sunset	5:42 p.m.	5:46 p.m.	5:52 p.m.	5:58 p.m.	6:04 p.m.
Daylight	10 hr 14 min	10 hr 18 min	10 hr 24 min	10 hr 31 min	10 hr 40 min

Average Monthly Precipitation—2.07 inches

January

Feathered Winter Visitors

Like many people from northern climates, there are several bird species that arrive in Central Texas to spend the winter. Three of the most notable are the American Robin (*Turdus migratorius*), the Cedar Waxwing (*Bombycilla cedrorum*), and the American Kestrel (*Falco sparverius*).

The largest of our thrushes, the well-known American Robin is gray-brown above, with a brick-red breast, white belly, and black-streaked white throat. Like all thrushes, it is one of our best singers (*cheerily cheer-up cheerio!*), and was named by homesick colonists for the robin that occurs commonly across Europe. The two are only distantly related, but both have red breasts. Robins withdraw from the northern portion of their range in winter and migrate southward to seek more abundant food supplies. They winter throughout Texas, but remain to breed primarily in the northern and eastern portions of the state and locally in the mountains of the west. On their southern wintering grounds here in Central Texas, they congregate in huge flocks, feeding together mostly on berries, and roosting en masse in trees at night. Earthworms are an important food source during their breeding season, and because they forage for worms largely on suburban lawns, they are vulnerable to pesticide poisoning and can be an important indicator of chemical pollution.

Gray-brown overall, with a crest on top of the head, a black mask edged in white, and yellow tips on its tail feathers, the Cedar Waxwing is a beautiful medium-sized songbird. Gregarious and often flying in flocks, its calls sound like very high-pitched *bzeee* notes. The waxwing gets its name from the waxy red appendages found in variable numbers on the tips of the secondary wing feathers of most birds. Waxwings with orange instead of yellow tail tips began appearing in the United States in the 1960s as a result of a red pigment picked up by the birds from eating the berries of an introduced (non-native) species of

An American Robin drinks from a rain puddle.

honeysuckle. One of the few temperate dwelling birds that are "frugivorous" or specializing in eating fruit, waxwings swallow berries whole. They can survive for months on fruit alone, and unlike many birds that regurgitate seeds from the fruit they eat, waxwings ingest and then defecate fruit seeds. Like American Robins, waxwings are also vulnerable to alcohol intoxication and even death after eating fermented fruit!

A robin-sized falcon, the American Kestrel is a gorgeous bird of prey with a sharp, hooked bill and talon-tipped feet ideal for hunting. Sometimes called a "sparrow hawk," the male kestrel is a rust-colored bird with slate blue wings and an unbarred tail while the female, the larger of the two, sports a barred tail and lacks the slate blue on the wings. Both possess a white face with two black streaks. Typically, it is the larger female kestrel that arrives on its wintering grounds ahead of the male, which allows her to select preferred habitats, so when the smaller males arrive they must take secondary locations. They utilize open fields and other grassy areas with perches from which they can watch for prey such as flying insects, bats, mice, small birds and reptiles. They can hover in mid-air while searching for prey and "kite" against the wind, flying at an appropriate speed facing the wind so they can stay in place.

A female American Kestrel, showing her rufous back with dark brown barring.

A Cedar Waxwing sits in an Ashe Juniper tree.

As you enjoy a brisk winter walk in your neighborhood and surrounding areas, keep an eye out for these common but attractive "winter Texans."

Birding Resources

■ Interested in learning more about birds? A great resource is the Travis Audubon Society, or TAS (www.travisaudubon.org). A local chapter of the National Audubon Society, their mission is to "promote the enjoyment, understanding, and conservation of native birds and their habitats." Get involved through membership events, volunteering, field trips, and classes. A local birding hotspot is Hornsby Bend Bird Observatory, or HBBO (www.hornsbybend.org), located at Austin Water Utility's Hornsby Bend Biosolids Management Plant, home of the famous Dillo Dirt. A "cooperative partnership promoting the study and understanding of birds in Central Texas," Hornsby Bend offers a host of public education, research, and monitoring opportunities.

- ❖ For waxwings and robins, check any location with a concentration of berry or fruit-producing shrubs and trees, such as the parking lot at the Westlake Village Shopping Center, the Hike & Bike Trail at Lady Bird Lake along Caesar Chavez, and the trails at the Lady Bird Johnson Wildflower Center.
- ❖ Kestrels prefer to perch on power lines above large, open, grassy areas like those along Platt Lane, Decker Lane, and MLK Boulevard towards Webberville.

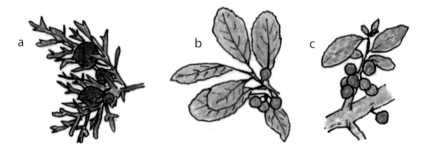

Berries for wildlife: Ashe Juniper (a), Possumhaw (b), and Yaupon (c).

The Cunning Coyote

Although the Coyote (*Canis latrans*) has been (and continues to be) one of the most persecuted mammals in human history, this is largely due to widespread, common misconceptions and myths that surround the species. Add the fact that they are a highly intelligent animal with keen senses of hearing, sight, and smell, and you can easily see why they are the subject of such scrutiny.

About the size of a small German shepherd, the Coyote weighs an average of 25 to 40 pounds, with long, slender legs, a bushy tail with a black tip, and large ears that are held erect. While its coat can vary, it is usually gray or buff-colored and its snout is long and slender. A strong swimmer, the Coyote characteristically runs with its tail down, instead of horizontally like foxes or up like wolves and dogs. Primarily nocturnal and very opportunistic, Coyotes will eat almost anything, but in Central Texas they prefer rabbits, rodents, and insects. Because Coyotes can utilize many different food sources and humans have all but exterminated its main predator, the wolf, Coyotes have rapidly spread to all parts of the country, including urban and suburban areas.

Considered monogamous with pairs living together for several years, Coy-

Coyotes can be seen at night or during the daytime.

otes are usually shy and elusive, but are frequently seen individually, in pairs, or in small groups, especially when near food. A family group, more commonly known as a pack, consists of the parents, their pups, and occasionally, the previous year's pups. Male and female Coyotes pair up, establish a territory, and breed from mid-January to early March. Normally utilizing a natural cavity or a den dug by another mammal, they will make the necessary renovations by excavating multiple escape tunnels linked to the surface. After a gestation period of 63–65 days, a litter of five to seven pups is born. During the weeks following the birth, the male will bring food to the family, but the female will not allow him inside the den. Coyotes normally live from 10 to 12 years.

It is easy to get the impression that an area is overflowing with Coyotes when one hears a family's howls. In reality, there are probably only 2–6 individuals in a pack. While some people may find it a bit unnerving, Coyotes use

January 5

Coyote Persecution

■ Coyotes have faced centuries of relentless persecution, hunted and trapped for their pelts or to protect ranching and farming interests. Research shows that lethal Coyote control is ineffective in the long run, and when left alone, they can easily regulate their numbers. By killing unwary Coyotes, humans have provided this species with only the best genetic material to deal with the technology we throw at them. As a result, the Coyote has come back to places and expanded its range into suburban and even some urban areas. Nothing has been gained by the massive programs put in place to suppress this species, and this vicious cycle can only be broken by a different force—one of reason and a change in mindset.

howling as a means of communication to tell non-family members to stay out of their territory, to locate one another within their territory, to distract other Coyotes away from young pups, and as a means for older pups to practice mimicking their parents.

Due to misconceptions and fears about Coyotes, many people don't recognize the beneficial aspects that Coyotes contribute to our ecosystem. Predators such as the Coyote, serve a valuable function in keeping prey species in balance with their habitat. Populations of small animals, such as rodents and insects, could increase out of control without these predators. Coyotes can reduce the number of small animals that homeowners and gardeners consider as pests. While Coyotes may change ecological balances of predator and prey species somewhat, they will not eliminate other species from the environment. Many scavenger animals, such as foxes and vultures, benefit from Coyote predation on other animals through increased food availability from leftover carcasses.

Coyotes are naturally afraid of people and their presence alone is not a cause for concern, though they can become habituated to rely on human-related sources of food. Simple steps you can take to peacefully coexist with them include keeping your garbage and recycling inside and secure until the morning of pickup, closing off crawlspaces under porches and decks, feeding your pets indoors, keeping your pets indoors at night (especially cats and small dogs), and educating your neighbors to do the same.

Like all wild animals, Coyotes have a right to inhabit our wild places, including the preserves that border our suburban homes and neighborhoods. If

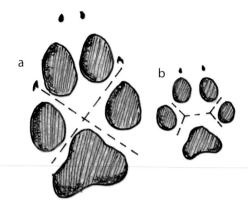

Canine tracks. The "negative space" between the toe pads forms an "X" for a Coyote (a), and an "H" for a Gray Fox (b).

you do your part to help strike a proactive balance between humans and these wild creatures and respect their right to exist, you may well be rewarded with a familial chorus of eerie howls on a moonlit night.

WHERE TO WATCH:

❖ More often heard than seen and active mainly at night, Coyotes can be found in open spaces that border our urban and suburban neighborhoods, such as Barton Creek Greenbelt, Bull Creek Preserve, Wild Basin, and Emma Long (City) Park.

❖ Get a close-up look at a Coyote at the Austin Nature & Science Center (ANSC).

There's No Such Thing as Buzzards

To most Texans, vultures are simply "buzzards," an unfortunate misnomer that stems from the term early settlers used to describe these birds that reminded them of a common, medium-sized hawk found in Europe. American vultures have their own distinct family and differ from vultures found on other continents, which are more closely related to hawks and eagles.

Vultures are characterized by small, unfeathered heads and hooked beaks, which help them feed on the carrion that makes up most of their diet. As scavengers, they often feed together and assemble in large groups to roost at night. These normally social birds become solitary during the spring nesting season, from March to June in Central Texas, and prefer protected rock ledges, caves, hollow trees, and even deserted buildings as nesting sites, as they do little to no nest construction. Male and female vultures look alike, and they have no song or call, although they will grunt and hiss when feeding or frightened.

Turkey Vultures (*Cathartes aura*) are one of two vulture species common in the Austin area. Large, sleek, and black with a naked red head, white beak, and longish tail, the Turkey Vulture has a six-foot wing span. Combined with its relatively light weight, you will often see this bird using thermals to carry it aloft, soaring high above the ground in sweeping circles. From below, its slender wings appear two-toned, with leading edge black wing linings contrasting with trailing edge light gray flight feathers. Unlike other vultures, the Turkey Vulture uses its sense of smell to locate carrion. And like its stork relatives, this vulture often defecates on its own legs, using the evaporation of the water in its feces to cool itself down.

Smaller, with a shorter tail, naked black head, and a wing span of less than five feet, the Black Vulture (*Coragyps atratus*) is not built for endless soaring like the Turkey Vulture. As such, you will often see this bird alternate rapid flapping of its wings with short glides. From below, its wings also appear two-toned, but with the light gray feathers appearing only on the wing tips. Unlike the Turkey Vulture, the Black Vulture will supplement its carrion diet with small mammals, reptiles, and young birds, and depends solely on its vision to find food. A more aggressive bird, Black Vultures will frequently form small groups and gang up on a larger Turkey Vulture to drive it from a carcass. But when threatened, it often regurgitates its stomach contents.

A Turkey Vulture sunning its wings.

A Black Vulture keeps a sharp eye out for its next meal.

Populations of Turkey and Black Vultures fluctuate throughout the year in Central Texas. Although some stay year-round, many Turkey Vultures spend the winter in Central America. Black Vultures also migrate, and may travel as far south as Brazil for the winter. Protected by the Migratory Bird Treaty Act of 1918, it is illegal to take, kill, or possess Turkey or Black vultures (or even possess a feather), except for those with the authority to care for birds that are injured and unable to return to the wild.

The Mexican Eagle

■ Often called the "Mexican Eagle," the Crested Caracara (*Caracara cheriway*) looks like a vulture but in fact is part of the falcon family. A large, long-legged bird with a black cap/crest, white throat and neck barred with black, bare red skin on the face, and white tail tipped in black, it also shows white patches at the ends of dark wings while in flight. While its northernmost range includes South-Central Texas, it is a common bird throughout most of Mexico, Central America, and northern South America. A bird of open country, it is usually seen with vultures feeding on carrion, but will also eat insects and small mammals.

A noble Crested Caracara at the Austin Nature & Science Center.

a

b

When in flight and observed from below, Turkey Vultures (a) show light feathers along the length of the wings, and Black Vultures (b) show light feathers at the wingtips.

While vultures may not be the most attractive bird around, you have to admire their majestic stature, graceful flight, unique social characteristics, and the key role they play as nature's best recyclers.

WHERE TO WATCH:

❖ More often than not, vultures are seen soaring along highways such as Loop 360, RM 2222, and US 183, looking for carrion (roadkill).

❖ Vultures roost in groups and can be found in fairly large numbers on power/ transmission towers in many areas of the city.

Dabblers and Divers

Wintertime is the perfect time to look for ducks in Central Texas. Several species that breed far north of our state's border return to Texas in the colder months to feed in our unfrozen freshwater lakes and rivers. From the Old English *duce,* the word duck is a derivative of the verb meaning to duck or dive, or bend down low as if to get under something. It best describes the way many ducks feed, by upending or diving under the water in search of a wide variety of food sources, such as small aquatic plants, grasses, fish, insects, amphibians, worms and mollusks. Most ducks fall into either the dabbler or diver category. Dabblers feed on the surface of the water, and sometimes on land, while divers disappear completely beneath the surface and forage deep underwater. In general, divers are heavier than dabblers, giving them the ability to submerge more easily, but they often pay the price by having more difficulty when taking off to fly.

The most distinctive dabbling duck is the Northern Shoveler (*Anas clypeata*). True to its name, it possesses a large, 2 1/2 inch long shovel-like bill, which is spoon-shaped and has a comb-like structure at its edges called a "pectin." The pecten is used to filter food from the water, and as an aid in preening its feathers. A medium-sized duck, the adult male (or drake) has an iridescent green head, rusty sides, and a white chest. When flushed from her nest, the adult female (or hen) will often defecate on the eggs, presumably to deter predators from eating them. This species of duck is monogamous, and stays together longer than any other known pairs of dabbling duck species.

Another common dabbler is the American Wigeon (*Anas americana*), the population of which is increasing throughout its range. The male has a white crown, green face patch, large white patches in its wings, and a black rear end bordered by white. At one time this duck was known as "baldpate" because the white crown resembles a man's bald head. Its feeding behavior is distinctive among the dabbling ducks, as its short bill allows it to be much more efficient at plucking vegetation from both the water and sometimes even agricultural fields. The diet of this duck includes a much higher proportion of plant matter than any other dabbler species.

Among the most abundant and widespread freshwater diving ducks is the Lesser Scaup (*Aythya affinis*). The male has a slight bump or peak on the back of the head, a bluish bill with a small black tip, light gray sides (black on the ends with white in the middle), and a black head, chest, and rear end. When grasped by a predator like a gray fox, an adult Lesser Scaup may play

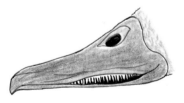

▲ *Typical duck bill, showing the "pectin" (from the Latin for "comb"), or structures used to strain food from the water and to aid in preening.*

◀ *The Northern Shoveler is named for its large bill.*

dead, rendering itself immobile with its head extended, eyes open, and wings folded close to its body. They are capable of diving underwater the day they are hatched, but are too buoyant to stay under for long, until maturity gives them the body composition and strength they need to stay underwater for longer periods of time.

Usually found on smaller, calmer bodies of water like ponds, Ring-necked Ducks (*Aythya collaris*) are more readily identified by the bold white ring around their bill than the subtle purplish band around their necks for which they are named. A medium-sized diving duck, they also have a small bump or peak on the back of their black heads, with the male having a black chest, back, and rear end, with gray sides and a white stripe up the shoulder.

The next time you visit a lake, river, or pond this winter, venture out to the quiet corners to see if you can spot one of our best known dabblers or divers.

Coots & Cormorants

■ Other inhabitants of wetlands and open bodies of water are the American Coot (*Fulica americana*) and the Double-crested Cormorant (*Phalacrocorax auritus*). Dark gray to black with yellow legs and a white beak with a white frontal shield, coots are often mistaken for ducks but are members of the rail family. In Texas year-round, their feet are lobed not webbed, and their bills resemble that of a chicken. Cormorants are large, dark water birds with long necks and bodies and medium-sized bills hooked at the tip. Common in Texas in the winter, they have a yellow-orange throat pouch and fly with their necks kinked. Both coots and cormorants dive underwater in search of food.

The American Coot is also called a "mud hen."

Double-crested Cormorants like to perch in bare trees.

Lesser Scaups, like this one, prefer sheltered freshwater whereas Greater Scaups (Aythya marila) *prefer open salt water.*

Small groups of Gadwall (Anas strepera) *are common on winter ponds and lakes.*

Another diving duck you are likely to see in winter is the Ruddy Duck (Oxyura jamaicensis).

WHERE TO WATCH:

❖ Local lakes where ducks congregate include Lady Bird Lake (especially at the junction with Barton Creek), Walter E. Long (Decker) Lake, and Lake Austin at the base of Mansfield Dam.

❖ Ducks are also fond of quiet waters provided by human-made ponds such as those at Hornsby Bend and Walnut Creek wastewater treatment plants, and the ponds at Riata, the Triangle, and Central Market.

A short winter storm leaves a dusting of snow on the oak-juniper woodlands.

CLIMATIC DATA FOR THE MONTH OF FEBRUARY IN AUSTIN.

	February 1	*February 7*	*February 14*	*February 21*	*February 28*
Record High	83°F	83°F	85°F	99°F	89°F
Average High	62°F	63°F	65°F	67°F	69°F
Average Low	41°F	42°F	44°F	45°F	47°F
Record Low	12°F	15°F	12°F	26°F	23°F
Sunrise	7:22 a.m.	7:18 a.m.	7:12 a.m.	7:05 a.m.	6:58 a.m.
Sunset	6:08 p.m.	6:13 p.m.	6:19 p.m.	6:24 p.m.	6:29 p.m.
Daylight	10 hr 46 min	10 hr 55 min	11 hr 7 min	11 hr 19 min	11 hr 31 min

Average Monthly Precipitation—2.34 inches

February

Winged Denizens of the Night

Owls have fascinated humans from time immemorial—to some cultures they are symbols of wisdom, while to others they are harbingers of doom and death. Adding to the mystique of these creatures is that they are mainly active at night, using their exceptional vision and acute hearing while flying silently through the dark, stealthily hunting down their prey.

A large round head and huge forward-facing eyes are features that make an owl instantly recognizable from other birds of prey. They have a sharp, downward-facing beak, strong talons, and soft, mottled plumage that allows them to blend into their natural surroundings. Although males and females are generally similar in appearance, the female is often 25 percent larger.

Like snakes, owls often eat their prey whole. Unlike snakes, the enzymes and acids that are present in the digestive tract of owls (and other birds of prey) do not digest the entire meal. Owls form undigested fur, bones, feathers, and other parts of prey into wet, slimy pellets. Approximately 20 hours after eating, they regurgitate a single pellet. Owl pellets are natural teaching tools that illustrate how the food chain works. Collectors sell them to specialty businesses, where they are sterilized and then sold to researchers and educators around the country.

Common in Central Texas, the Eastern Screech-Owl (*Megascops asio*) is found in wooded suburban and rural areas and readily nests in tree cavities as well as human-made nest boxes. A small owl 6 to 10 inches in length with a wingspan of 19 to 24 inches, it has feathered ear tufts and is normally gray, brownish-gray, or less commonly reddish-brown. The Eastern Screech-Owl eats a variety of small animals, and each night consumes from one-quarter to one-third of its own body weight, sometimes skipping a night to store food instead. It uses a soft trilling call to keep in contact with a mate or family

An Eastern Screech-Owl at dusk, awakening from its roost.

members, and the male's trill can advertise a nest site when courting a female or signal an arrival at the nest with food. This owl also has a descending whinny, which is used to defend its territory. Often heard calling to each other this time of year, Eastern Screech-Owl pairs are usually monogamous and remain together for life, although they will readily take a new mate when one dies. By mid-April, the female lays three to four eggs on average, and the downy white owlets emerge from the nest by mid-May.

Also common but much larger at 18 to 25 inches in length with a wingspan of 40 to 57 inches, the Great Horned Owl (*Bubo virginianus*) prefers habitats of secondary-growth woodlands mixed with open meadows. Often found perching next to an open area—and even on rooftops and streetlamps—this owl often nests in tree hollows, broken off snags, or nests made by other large birds. It has prominent ear tufts spaced widely on its head, a brownish-gray body with dark barring, and a rusty facial disk edged in black surrounding each of its orange-yellow eyes. The Great Horned Owl has a broad diet of small mammals, birds, amphibians, and reptiles, and due to its exceptionally poor sense of smell, is the only animal that regularly eats skunks! It can take down large prey two to three times heavier than itself, and can even take other owls. Great Horned Owls have a large repertoire of sounds, but the most common is that of the male's resonant territorial call *hoo-hoo hoooooo hoo-hoo* that can be heard over several miles through the canyons on a still night. Nesting season is in January or February, when males and females hoot to each other. Typically two to four eggs are laid and incubated solely by the female, until the young start roaming from the nest six to seven weeks later. Families remain loosely associated during the summer before the young disperse in the fall. Adults tend to remain near their breeding areas year-round, while the juveniles can disperse up to 150 miles. Territories are maintained by the same pair for as many as eight consecutive years; however, these owls are solitary in nature, only staying with their mate during the nesting season.

▲ *Owl primary flight feathers (not to scale): Great Horned Owl (a), and Eastern Screech-Owl (b).*

◀ *A Great Horned Owl at the Austin Nature & Science Center.*

Owl Nest Box Placement

■ Nest box placement for Eastern Screech-Owls is important, and depends on a few key factors:

- the rooftop should be 10 feet or more off the ground
- the box can face any direction but north (this is where the cold weather winds come from)
- select a more open side of a tree where the owl does not have to fly through leaves and branches, and preferably on the main trunk under a large limb to help keep rain off the box
- if possible, mount the box on a hardwood tree (oak, pecan, etc.) or a juniper, but only if it is a mature tree and not a dense thicket

For more information, and a great place to buy owl boxes made from new and retired fence wood, try Owl Shack (www.owlshack.com).

No other bird family has aroused more universal fascination and interest than that of the owl. Listen and look for these magical creatures if you're out and about in your neighborhood, especially in the late night hours and just before dawn.

WHERE TO WATCH:

❖ Both Eastern Screech and Great Horned Owls frequent our suburban neighborhoods, with screech owls often inhabiting artificial owl nest boxes, and both owls can be seen close-up at the Austin Nature and Science Center.

Cat Tracks

Of the 36 species of wild cats in the world, seven species roam North America, and only two range widely in the state of Texas. In the desert mountain ranges of West Texas, the dense brushlands of the Rio Grande Valley, and parts of the Edwards Plateau in Central Texas, the Mountain Lion (*Puma concolor*) is the top predator. Preferring heavily wooded uplands and bottomland forests, as well as the rocky limestone regions of the Edwards Plateau, the Bobcat (*Lynx rufus*) is present throughout Texas.

A large, long-tailed, unspotted cat, the Mountain Lion has a lithe, muscular body covered in short, tawny fur with darker markings on the face, ears, and tip of the tail. Also known as the Cougar or Puma, Mountain Lions can run up to 43 miles per hour, leap 20 feet from a standing position, and jump a vertical distance of 16 feet! Unlike other big cats, they cannot roar, but they do purr like their close relative, the house cat. They can grow up to 8 feet long, weigh

up to 150 pounds, and can kill prey to up seven times their body weight. Their diet consists chiefly of large and small mammals, and although mainly solitary, they will come together to mate.

A medium-sized cat with a spotted and barred gray to reddish brown coat, black-tufted ears, and a stubby tail, the Bobcat inhabits more of North America than any other wild native feline. With its flexible body measuring up to 3 feet long and weighing up to 30 pounds, it also depends on surprise to ambush and kill its prey. It prefers to eat a wide variety of small mammals and is more of a generalist predator than its larger relative the Mountain Lion. While the Bobcat is highly adaptable and in most areas has learned to cope with the inroads of human settlement, both the Bobcat and the Mountain Lion face threats due to hunting by humans as well as from habitat loss and fragmentation. Little has been learned about these wild cats due to their stealth and mainly nocturnal habits, and while fairly common, they leave scant evidence of their presence. Often, the only evidence that presents itself is a set of tracks.

While the front tracks of felines (such as Mountain Lions and Bobcats) and canines (such as Coyotes and foxes) are larger than the hind tracks, there are some key differences that can aid in proper identification. Cat tracks do not usually have claw marks because their claws are retractable and only show

A regal Mountain Lion at the Austin Zoo.

A Bobcat peers out from his protected perch.

when they are pouncing or running. In terms of their palm pad, cats have three lobes on the hind edge and two lobes on the leading edge, where dogs have two lobes on the hind edge and one lobe on the leading edge. Lastly, the two front middle toe pads of a cat are not aligned as they are in a dog track, and the positioning of the leading toe pad can help you identify a left from a right foot. If the toe that is furthest forward is on the right, the track is made by the left foot,

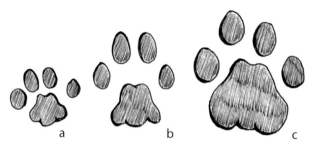

Tracks made by the right front paw of feline species: Housecat (a), Bobcat (b), and Mountain Lion (c).

Casting Tracks

▪ Being a good steward of nature means leaving things as you found them, but you can bring a piece of nature home by casting an animal track. Here's how:

- Look for a nicely formed track, preferably in a firm substrate such as dried mud. Carefully remove any debris.
- Use a can (with both ends removed) or a piece of cardboard held together with a paper clip as a form and place the form around the track.
- With a Ziploc bag and a spoon, mix together a 2 to 1 ratio of Plaster of Paris and water.
- The plaster mixture sets up quickly, so immediately pour it into the form on the side of the track, and let it ooze onto the track. Fill the form with about 1 inch of plaster.
- Lightly tap on the top of the plaster surface to bring up any bubbles from within and allow for a better cast. Leave it to dry for about 1 hour.
- After one hour, carefully lift both the cast and the form (still together) from opposite sides of the form and place it in a baggie to take home.
- Once at home, take it out of the baggie, and after an additional 24 hours of drying, separate the cast from the form.
- Clean off any dirt by washing the cast under running water. Paint or leave natural, and enjoy!

and if it is on the left, the track is made by the right foot. Needless to say, the tracks of a Mountain Lion are generally larger than that of a Bobcat, roughly 3–4 inches wide versus 2–3 inches wide. However, a large Bobcat can splay its foot over 3 inches, and in those rarer cases the size of the palm pad is used to determine which feline left the tracks.

While you may never actually see a Mountain Lion or Bobcat in Central Texas, you can be sure these magnificent mammals are present. Tracks and signs are everywhere, and if you spend the time to study them, they can tell you much about the secret lives of these beautifully elusive felines.

WHERE TO WATCH:

❖ While rarely sighted in the wild, Mountain Lions can be seen at the Austin Zoo, and a Bobcat is resident at the Austin Nature & Science Center.

A Bird That Prefers to Run

Spend any amount of time in Texas or the Southwestern United States and you'll undoubtedly spot the Greater Roadrunner (*Geococcyx californianus*), a long-legged, ground-dwelling member of the cuckoo family. It is regionally called *paisano,* the Spanish word for "constant friend" or "compatriot." This large chicken-like bird, with its long tail and shaggy crest, is fully capable of flying, but usually runs instead, at speeds up to 18 miles per hour. True to its name, a group of these birds is known as a "marathon" or a "race" of roadrunners.

A Greater Roadrunner with crest raised, dashing across an open field.

From a behavioral point of view, the roadrunner is a fascinating subject. This signature bird of the southwest slows its bodily functions at night, and conserves body heat by lowering its temperature and becoming lethargic. In the early morning, it can warm itself up without expending a lot of energy. Turning its back to the sun, it erects its feathers to expose an underlying patch of black skin between its wings that helps it quickly absorb more solar energy. When running at top speed, it holds its head and tail flat and parallel to the ground.

The Greater Roadrunner is an opportunistic forager, and while it can catch small birds at feeders and nest boxes, more often it eats a variety of fruits, seeds, as well as venomous prey items, including large insects, spiders, scorpions, and even rattlesnakes. Surprisingly agile, two birds will frequently cooperate to kill a large snake, taking turns to distract it, pin its head with their heavy bill, and beat it against a rock or the ground. When alarmed or curious, the roadrunner raises its crest and white-edged tail, and utters a series of coos or rapidly clatters its beak.

A Greater Roadrunner with his lizard catch, used to attract a mate.

Living in dry, open habitats, the roadrunner has adapted by developing salt glands in front of its eyes to excrete excess salt from its blood. While these glands are more common in ocean-going birds that drink seawater, they enable the roadrunner to go without drinking water as long as it eats food with high moisture content, but it will drink water if available. When courting season begins in late February, many male roadrunners attract a female with cooing calls and then offer her food, usually in the form of a dead lizard. If the female accepts, copulation occurs, during which the food is often exchanged.

In a small tree, scrubby bush, or a stand of cactus, both parents build a shallow platform of thorny sticks, line it with leaves, grass, feathers, and occasionally shed snake skins. Clutch size can vary from two to six eggs, depending on the food supply. If all the eggs do not hatch at roughly the same time (called asynchronous hatching), and the food supply declines during the breeding season, the parents may eat the younger chicks or feed them to their older siblings. In times of abundant food, roadrunners will double-brood, or raise a second family just as soon as the first is out of the nest.

Greater Roadrunner populations appear stable across their range, and are seen in the Austin area year-round. However, like most species, they tend to disappear when their habitat is fragmented by development.

WHERE TO WATCH:

❖ While they can be seen in virtually every habitat in Austin, Greater Roadrunners prefer open, grassy areas and can most often be observed on the wide shoulders of roadways such as Loop 360, FM 620, and State Highway 71.

Fronds of Ferns

More often associated with mossy, moist, old-growth forests in the Northeast or Northwest, many are surprised to learn that ferns do exist in Texas. In fact, unlike other western states, Texas has a large and varied set of fern flora, although they are mostly concentrated in three regions: the Trans-Pecos of West Texas, the Edwards Plateau of Central Texas, and the Pineywoods of East Texas.

Ferns are a fascinating subject, due to their ancient lineage and distinct biology. The oldest fossil remains of ferns have been dated to 250 million years ago, and they were at their height, both literally and figuratively, during the Carboniferous Period. Many species were tree-like, but the ferns of today are herbaceous and much smaller in stature. Fern structure includes the root, also known as rootstock or rhizome, the stalk or stem, and the fronds, also known as leaves or blades.

February 23

Differing from flowering plants because they reproduce not by seeds but through spores, fronds of ferns can be fertile or sterile. Only the fertile ones produce the spores, which are formed in groups of four and are most often found clustered on the back of the fronds. These clusters are called "sporangia," and their patterned arrangement is usually associated with the veins in the frond. In return for their reproductive ability, the fern provides each group of sporangia a "sorus," or distinct protective covering. The branching and shape of the fronds, the shape, size, and placement of the spores, as well as the shape of the protective covering are the features most used in fern identification. While most ferns in the Austin area are sporiferous somewhat later in the year, many are still quite noticeably verdant in the late winter landscape.

One of the most common ferns found on the Edwards Plateau is the Purple Cliffbrake (*Pellaea atropurpurea*). Rather small and evergreen, its Greek name means "dusky" and refers to the dark stems. This fern prefers rock ledges, cliffs, and canyon walls, seemingly growing out of rock in partially shady areas. It is sporiferous from March to November. Often associated with the Purple Cliffbrake is the Alabama Lipfern (*Cheilanthes alabamensis*). Also common, this fern is found on shady, protected calcareous rock slopes, ledges, and cliffs. Small and evergreen, its Greek name refers to the "lip-like" shape of the spore covering. Alabama Lipfern is sporiferous most of the year, but mainly from March to November.

Southern Maidenhair (*Adiantum capillus-veneris*) is a delicate rock-inhabiting fern of shady stream banks and moist wooded slopes, usually growing in seepage along streams and in canyons. Its ancient Greek name means

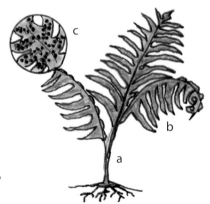

Basic fern anatomy: stalk, (a), frond (b), and sporangia (c).

Purple Cliffbrake is a fern with dusky-colored stems.

"unwetted," relating to the foliage being repellent to raindrops. Sporiferous from May to January, it has fine, lacy foliage, giving it a delicate, graceful character. Growing from 6 inches to 1 foot high, this fern goes dormant during droughts. Almost always associated with Southern Maidenhair, Wood Fern (*Thelypteris kunthii),* is also known as River Fern or Southern Shield Fern. The latter name comes from the shield-shaped membrane covering the spores. This fern is found on the shady edge of sandy creeks, low woods, deep canyons, and especially at the base of dripping limestone bluffs. Sporiferous from April to November, this semi-evergreen fern has gracefully arching fronds that grow up to 3 feet, and take on a bronze color as winter approaches.

Ferns drop millions, if not billions of spores during their lifetime, and while many can be carried great distances through air currents, very few ever land in spots suitable for growth. While well-understood, the lifecycle of ferns is quite complicated. Even today, those who study ferns can agree on four main classes of ferns, but debate still exists on which are true ferns and which are fern allies. Regardless of their classification, one can still enjoy their mysterious nature and lush beauty.

Southern Maidenhair fern dripping from a rock ledge.

Wood Fern, also known as River or Southern Shield Fern.

Fern Symbolism

■ Rich with symbolism and meaning, the fern is an ancient image. Many believe that within its graceful fronds lies the deep wisdom of Mother Earth, both literally as a medicinal plant, and figuratively as a multi-cultural symbol. Early people thought that ferns brought rain, protection, sincerity, confidence, shelter, and magic. New leaves, expanding by the unrolling of a tight spiral called a fiddlehead or "crozier," are like a consciousness awakening. Also known as the "koru" to the indigenous peoples of New Zealand and represented as a spiral, the fiddlehead symbolizes new life, new beginnings, and the bringing of purity to the world. When represented by more than one frond, it symbolizes the strength of a relationship or family and signifies the bonding of two disparate lives.

WHERE TO WATCH:

❖ Purple Cliffbrake and Alabama Lipfern grow on limestone hillsides in areas like Turkey Creek Trail in Emma Long Park, Bull Creek Preserve, and St. Edwards Park.

❖ Look for Southern Maidenhair growing on damp cliff faces along Barton Creek Greenbelt, Hamilton Pool, and Westcave Preserve, while Wood Ferns can be frequently found in damp hollows and creek bottoms of places such as Walnut Creek Metropolitan Park and Commons Ford Park.

The scientific name for this mushroom, Morchella esculenta, means "a morel that is good to eat," and they can often be found during a rainy spring.

CLIMATIC DATA FOR THE MONTH OF MARCH IN AUSTIN.

	March 1	March 7	March 14	March 21	March 28
Record High	87°F	87°F	96°F	91°F	98°F
Average High	69°F	70°F	72°F	74°F	75°F
Average Low	47°F	49°F	51°F	52°F	54°F
Record Low	21°F	24°F	28°F	24°F	27°F
Sunrise	6:57 a.m.	6:50 a.m.	7:42 a.m.	7:34 a.m.	7:25 a.m.
Sunset	6:30 p.m.	6:34 p.m.	7:39 p.m.	7:43 p.m.	7:47 p.m.
Daylight	11 hr 33 min	11 hr 44 min	11 hr 57 min	12 hr 9 min	12 hr 22 min

Average Monthly Precipitation—2.32 inches

March

An Endangered Warbler

Tweeh-tweeh-tweeh-TWEEsy! Can you hear it? Early March marks the return of the Golden-cheeked Warbler (*Dendroica chrysoparia*), which spends its winters in the forests of Central America, and is present spring through late summer in fewer than 35 counties in Central Texas. Sadly, this unique bird is one of over 200 species of migratory birds whose survival is threatened by the destruction of native habitat—in both its winter and summer ranges—due to agriculture and development.

The Golden-cheeked Warbler is a 4 to 5 inch songbird with black to dark gray upperparts and white underparts with thick black streaks on its sides.

A male Golden-cheeked Warbler foraging high in a Texas Red Oak tree.

A male Golden-cheeked Warbler in an Ashe Juniper tree.

Its head has a black cap and throat, bright yellow cheeks, and a dark eye-line. Dark wings with two white wing bars complete the brightly colored male, while the female is duller overall with olive-green upperparts, a streaked cap, and a generally whiter throat.

This warbler is totally dependent on mixed woodlands consisting of oak and stands of old-growth Ashe Juniper (*Juniperus ashei*) for nesting habitat, just like those found in the ravines and canyons that surround our Austin neighborhoods. This unique habitat provides the warbler with long strips of peeling bark from the mature Ashe Juniper trees and they use them, along with spider webs and lichens, to construct their nests. An insect-eating bird, they forage through the leaves and bark of oaks and other trees, gleaning from them a multitude of caterpillars, spiders, beetles, and various insects.

Golden-cheeked Warblers arrive at their breeding grounds by mid-March, returning to virtually the same territories each year and nesting from April to May. Females lay three to four eggs during the nesting season, with the young fledgling birds leaving the nest only eight or nine days after hatching, staying in the vicinity of their caring parents. Of the nearly 360 bird species that breed

A prime example of mixed woodland Golden-cheeked Warbler habitat.

in Texas, the Golden-cheeked Warbler is the only one that nests exclusively in Texas, so each bird is a native Texan.

As previously mentioned, the major threat to the warbler is native habitat destruction and fragmentation, with the most significant factor being the widespread removal of native Ashe Junipers in Central Texas. Between the early 1970s and the 1990s, at least 50% of the warbler's habitat was lost to urbanization. The result was a dramatic decline in the

Summer breeding range for the Golden-cheeked Warbler in Central Texas.

Balcones Canyonlands Conservation Plan

■ On May 2, 1996, the City of Austin and Travis County were issued a regional permit by the U.S. Fish and Wildlife Service to create a preserve system to protect eight federally endangered species and 27 species of concern (believed to be at risk). Called the Balcones Canyonlands Conservation Plan (BCCP), this community-based solution sets aside these lands as mitigation for 'take,' or the removal of occupied endangered species habitat or species displacement due to development of existing habitat areas. The city, county, and the Lower Colorado River Authority (LCRA) can build new public schools, roads, and other infrastructure but only if they minimize the impact by:

- Assembling a minimum of 30,428 acres of endangered species habitat in western Travis County by 2016, known collectively as the Balcones Canyonlands Preserve (BCP), which also includes protection for karst (cave) features and rare plants
- Provide ongoing maintenance, patrolling, and biological management of BCP lands
- Support the BCCP permit terms and conditions by conducting biological monitoring and research activities

Currently the city, county, and LCRA have worked with non-profit conservation organizations and private landowners to secure over 92 percent of the required acreage for the BCP, one of our nation's largest urban preserves, which not only protects habitat but contributes to clean air, clean water, and the quality of life for all Central Texas residents. Learn more at www.co.travis.tx.us/tnr/bccp.

warbler's population—from more than 15,000 to fewer than 5,000—and its listing as an endangered species in the United States.

What can we do to preserve this unique Texas species for future generations? Buy shade-grown coffee, which supports better agricultural practices that protect habitat in the warbler's wintering range. Here at home, support the Balcones Canyonlands Preserve (BCP) System, which contains the greatest amount of prime warbler habitat in large, undisturbed tracts (from March 1 to July 31, the BCP is closed for the Golden-cheeked Warbler breeding season, and citizens must obtain a permit for access during this time). But most of all consider yourself lucky if you see a rare Golden-cheeked Warbler, and think twice before cutting down those native, life-sustaining Ashe Junipers.

WHERE TO WATCH:

❖ Hike along trails like Turkey Creek at Emma Long Park, Warbler Vista at Balcones Canyonlands National Wildlife Refuge, and in St. Edward's Park to listen and look for the Golden-cheeked Warbler.
❖ Sign up for a guided hike hosted by the City of Austin's Wildland Conservation Division on a Balcones Canyonlands Preserve (BCP) property.
❖ See also the Balcones Songbird Festival and the Vireo Viewing Stand referenced in the "The Song of the Vireo" section in the April chapter.

Beneficial Bats

For millions of years, bats have played essential roles in nature's system of checks and balances. Once extremely abundant, they dominated the night skies. In more in recent times, however, their declining numbers reflect the ongoing compromise of the overall health and stability of our environment.

Bats are mammals, but such unique ones that scientists have put them in their own group, the Chiroptera, or "hand-wings." Occupying a large variety of habitats ranging from desert communities through pinyon-juniper woodland and pine-oak forests, there are 26 species of bats known to occur in Texas, but none is more commonly seen in our area than the Mexican Free-tailed Bat (*Tadarida brasiliensis*). These bats migrate each spring from Central Mexico to the same areas in the Southwestern United States, with the densest concentrations occurring in Texas. In fact, it is estimated that 100 million come to Central Texas each year in March to raise their young. At approximately

A Mexican Free-tailed Bat emergence at Bracken Cave.

1.5 million individuals, the Mexican Free-tailed Bat colony living under the Congress Avenue Bridge in downtown Austin is the largest urban bat colony in the world!

Ranging from dark brown to gray, Mexican Free-tailed Bats are not much to look at, and some have described them as looking like "little gnomes with an overbite." They get their name from their tail, which protrudes freely beyond the wing membrane. But don't let their plain appearance fool you—these are the "speedsters of the bat world," and they have been clocked flying at 60 miles per hour using tail winds, and flying higher than any other bat at altitudes over 10,000 feet. Mexican Free-tailed Bats are mostly migratory, with their arrival beginning in late February and their departure

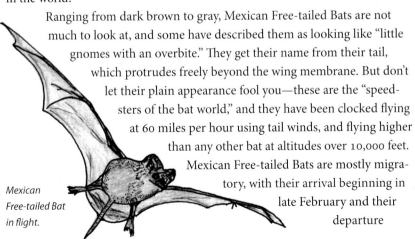

Mexican Free-tailed Bat in flight.

beginning in late October, triggered by the passage of strong cold fronts from the north. Not all bats leave, however, and for unknown reasons several thousand of them stay behind each winter.

Comprised mostly of females, the Austin bat colony sees an explosion of births in early June, when each female gives birth to a single baby bat, or pup. At birth they already weigh one-third of their mother's body weight, and are nursed by their mother who locates them among the thousands by each pup's distinctive voice and scent. In five weeks the pup learns to fly and begins hunting insects on its own. Aside from being fun to watch, bats make our world a better place to live. They are gentle and incredibly sophisticated animals, and on each nightly flight out from under the bridge, they consume between 1,000 and 2,000 tons of insects, including major agricultural pests.

Unfortunately, in spite of the popularity of the Austin bat colony, bats remain the world's most endangered and least appreciated animals. While bats suffer from environmental pollution and habitat loss like other wildlife, persecution from humans remains a primary cause for their decline. Their colonies represent the densest aggregations of mammals present in a limited number of locations, and combined with a low reproductive rate, recovery from the destruction of a large colony would be very slow. As such, it is important to preserve those colonies that still thrive, and with the help of organizations like Bat Conservation International and The Nature Conservancy, along with private landowners, this unique resource and their habitat can be protected.

Each summer night, when you join the hundreds of people gathered to watch the Mexican Free-tailed Bats emerge from their concrete roost in downtown Austin, you are witnessing one of nature's most wondrous spectacles.

Bat Conservation International

■ Bat Conservation International (BCI) is an Austin-based nonprofit devoted to "conservation, education, and research initiatives involving bats and the ecosystems they serve." In 1982, after scientists became concerned that bats, essential to the balance of nature and human economies, were in alarming decline, Dr. Merlin Tuttle formed BCI. Both bats and people have benefited from BCI's educational offerings and conservation efforts. To find out more, see www.batcon.org.

WHERE TO WATCH:

❖ At dusk, view a Mexican Free-tailed Bat emergence at the Congress Avenue Bridge in downtown Austin or at the McNeil Bridge over I-35 in Williamson County.

❖ For more bat viewing locations and opportunities, visit Bat Conservation International's website at www.batcon.org.

Not So Lonesome Doves

Often used as a symbol of peace, the dove, or *paloma* in Spanish, represents a family of birds that feeds chiefly on grain, other seeds, and fruit. Abundant and widespread, the larger species of these birds are usually called pigeons, while the doves are generally a bit smaller. In the Austin area, the most common doves are the White-winged (*Zenaida asiatica*), Mourning (*Zenaida macroura*), and Inca (*Columbina inca*), with the Eurasian Collared-Dove (*Streptopelia decaocto*) not far behind.

The heavy-bodied White-winged Dove has large white wing patches which show only as narrow bands of white on the folded wings of perching birds. Its shorter, rounded tail has broad white corners, the skin around its eye is a bright blue, its iris is red, and there is a black streak on its cheek. There are several variations of its loud, low-pitched cooing calls, the most frequent being interpreted as *who cooks for you?* White-wings breed several times during the April to September nesting season. They nest singly or in colonies, building crude stick structures to hold the two pale buff eggs that hatch after only two weeks of incubation.

In the late 1800s and early 1900s, accounts from settlers in Texas suggested that there were several million White-winged Doves in the Rio Grande Valley. However, with the mass destruction of their native scrub forest nesting habitat to make way for agriculture, the populations fell to several hundred thousand. The white-wing adapted by switching its nesting preference to citrus and other leafy trees, and the numbers have been rebounding ever since. Since agriculture in the Southwestern United States continues to provide year-round food and watering sources, it allows for ongoing expansion of this dove's range and enables more and more white-wings to overwinter rather than migrate seasonally.

While the White-winged Dove is native to parts of Texas, the Mourning Dove is the only native Texas bird that has been documented in all of the state's

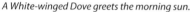

A White-winged Dove greets the morning sun.

An earlier name for the Mourning Dove was "moaning dove" due to its distinctive call.

254 counties. The trim-bodied Mourning Dove has a small, rounded head, slender neck, a blue ring around each eye, and wings that whistle in flight. Its tail is long and pointed, with white outer edges, and the adults have black spots on the upper wings. It has a low, mournful call *oowoo-woo-woo-woo* and like other doves, it is able to suck up water in its bill without raising its head to drink.

In Central Texas, the Mourning Dove can breed virtually year-round, with peak season between March and September. During nest-building, the female stays at the nest while the male collects sticks. He will stand on her back to give her the nest material, which she takes and weaves into the nest. After the female lays two eggs, the male usually incubates them from mid-morning to late afternoon, and the female the rest of the day and throughout the night.

A small tropical dove of arid areas, the Inca Dove has a light brown body with dark brown edging on its feathers that give it a scalloped appearance. Its

Inca Dove perched in a Texas Ash tree.

long tail has a square tip with white outer edges, and the rufous in its wings is visible during flight. The call of the Inca Dove is often translated as "no hope." The Inca Dove engages in an odd behavior called pyramid roosting. Pairs or groups of these doves may huddle together in the sunshine, with some sitting on the backs of others. The pyramid may be up to three layers high and include up to as many as 12 birds.

When talking about doves in Texas, mention must be made of the non-native Eurasian Collared-Dove. Introduced into the Bahamas in the mid-1970s from Europe (originally India), this dove has spread rapidly across much of North America. As its range expansion is still an evolving story, the extent of its final range and the impact it will have on other bird species remains to be seen. This large dove can be identified by its sandy gray body, long square tail with a broad white edge underneath, and a black half-collar on the back of the neck. Its song is a three note *coo-cooo-cup* and it makes a growling call in flight.

The increasingly common but non-native Eurasian Collared-Dove.

Although doves are a quintessential part of nature in Texas, as anyone who feeds wild birds knows, if you don't do your part to discourage them from your feeders, they'll be sure to eat you out of house and home.

To identify doves by ear, listen for the following:

- White-winged Doves have a drawn out, cooing call, that sounds like *who-cooks-for-you*, and their wings produce a weak whistle on takeoff, lower and softer than the Mourning Dove
- When taking off, the Mourning Dove's wings make a sharp whistling or whinnying sound, and their call is a mournful *oowoo-woo-woo-woo*, sometimes mistaken for an owl
- Inca Doves have a fairly high, forceful cooing call that sounds like *no-hope*, often repeated monotonously, and their wings produce a distinctively quiet, dry rattle upon takeoff
- Having no wing whistle in flight, the Eurasian Collared-Dove's song is a rhythmic, three-syllable *coo-cooo-cup*, steadily repeated and slightly lower pitched than the Mourning Dove

WHERE TO WATCH:

❖ All resident doves are found throughout the Austin area, and are frequently seen at backyard bird feeders, foraging on the ground, and perched on power lines or tree branches.

Relative sizes of our common doves. Inca (a), Mourning (b), White-winged (c), and Eurasian Collared (d).

Spiny Splendor

Often described as unusual and unique, cacti are a family of plants native only to the Americas, and due to its wide variety of habitats Texas has the most diverse cactus population of any state. In the Hill Country, cacti are abundant and some species are among the early bloomers that characterize the arrival of spring.

While all cacti are succulents, not all succulents are cacti. Cacti occur in various shapes and sizes. Anatomically speaking, cacti consist of tubercles, areoles, leaves, spines, glochids, and flowers. Tubercles refer to enlarged, nipple-shaped structures on the surface of the cactus. When running in vertical lines or aligned spirally along a stem, tubercles form ribs which can aid in species identification and add strength and stability to the body of the cactus. Each tubercle bears an areole, which is a highly specialized structure that can give rise to leaves, spines, flowers, fruits, or other stems. While cacti do not appear to have typical flat, green leaves, most have tiny ones that reduce the surface area through which cacti lose water. Spines are modified leaves and can vary in number, arrangement, size, and shape. Prickly Pears, or *Opuntia,* are the

General cactus shapes can help narrow down the search for proper identification: flat-segmented (a), round-segmented (b), cylindrical (c), and globular (d).

only family of cacti that have glochids, much shorter and thinner spines that dislodge easily and are difficult to remove from the skin.

Perhaps the most stunning feature of cacti is the strikingly beautiful flowers they produce. In proportion to the plant, the flower is generally quite large and can appear in every color except blue. Unlike other flowers, cactus flowers are "inside out," hollow tubes where the ovary is located internally beneath all other parts of the flower. Maturing from this floral ovary is the cactus fruit, which contains the seeds. These fruits, also called "tunas," are eaten by several species of mammals and birds, thereby ensuring distribution the seeds and propagation of the species.

By far the most common cactus in Central Texas is the Texas Prickly Pear (*Opuntia engelmannii* var. *lindheimeri*). A relatively large, sprawling plant, this cactus has green to blue-green pads, mostly yellow spines, and almost circular areoles. Brilliant yellow blooms appear in March through June, opening in the morning and afternoon, and sometimes closing at night. There are several species of prickly pear in Texas, another being the Brown-spined (*Opuntia phaeacantha*), and collectively they are considered the state plant of Texas.

Also called Christmas Cholla and Pencil Cactus, Tasajillo (*Cylindropuntia leptocaulis*) is a low shrub with pencil-sized branched stems. Its spines are gray tipped with yellow, growing out of broadly elliptical areoles. Small, pale green to yellowish-green blooms appear in March and continue through August, opening in late afternoon and closing at night.

The brilliant yellow flowers of the Texas Prickly Pear.

Brown-spined Prickly Pear flowers have a red center. They open in the afternoon and close at night.

With all but one protruding central spine forming a star at the areole, the Grooved Nipple Cactus (*Coryphantha sulcata*) is also known as the Finger Cactus and the Pineapple Cactus. Often seen in growing in clumps, its gray spines contrast with its green globular shape, and it blooms at the apex with a golden yellow flower from April through May.

Identified by radial spines in longitudinal rows along its columnar body, the Lace Cactus (*Echinocereus reichenbachii*) is prolific and probably one of the best known cacti in our area. Elliptical to linear areoles at the base of the spines are close enough together to cause the spines to overlap and mimic fine lace. Its bright pink to magenta flowers appear in April and June, but only last for a day.

While they can vary greatly in size and general appearance, cacti have played an important role in ancient civilizations. Tenochtitlan, the earlier name

The small greenish-yellow bloom of the Tasajillo.

The bright red fruits intermingled among the green stems of the Tasajillo give rise to its other common name, the Christmas Cholla.

of Mexico City, means "place of the sacred cactus." Images of this family of plants occur in many forms of historical art, emphasizing its important role in daily life by providing food, wood, fiber, and the spectacular beauty only a cactus bloom can bring.

Cochineal

■ Cochineal (*Dactylopius coccus*) is a scale insect most frequently found on the pads of prickly pear cactus and other cacti in the family that contains the genus *Opuntia*. The insect covers itself in a waxy white substance to reduce moisture loss and protect itself from the sun. It feeds on plant moisture and nutrients, and in turn produces carminic acid, the primary ingredient for carmine dye. Mainly extracted from the female insects, this natural crimson dye was used by the Aztec and Mayan peoples to color textiles. A few centuries ago, production of this dye grew rapidly, and it soon became Mexico's second most valued export after silver. Traded to India, Spain, and other parts of Europe, cochineal dye was so highly prized that its price was regularly quoted on the Amsterdam and London Commodity Exchanges. After synthetic dyes were invented in the late nineteenth century, the production of cochineal dye greatly diminished. However, recent health fears over artificial ingredients have caused resurgence in cochineal dye production once again, and it can be found in many cosmetics and as a food additive under names like cochineal extract, carmine, crimson lake, and natural red 4. Today, major producers include Peru, the Canary Islands, Chile, and Mexico.

Cochineal on prickly pear pads.

The short-lived magenta flower of the Lace Cactus.

Grooved Nipple Cactus blooms may remain open for two to three days.

WHERE TO WATCH:

❖ Prickly pear cactus species and Tasajillo are quite common, and can be found in most all undisturbed natural areas as well as planted landscapes such as Zilker Gardens and the Lady Bird Johnson Wildflower Center.

❖ Grooved Nipple Cactus and Lace Cactus are less common but may be found in rocky limestone in wild areas such as Bull Creek Preserve, St. Edward's Park, and Wild Basin.

*Suspended by a forked twig, the White-eyed Vireo's (*Vireo griseus*) nest is made up of twigs, grass, bark strips, and leaves bound with spider silk.*

April

CLIMATIC DATA FOR THE MONTH OF APRIL IN AUSTIN.

	April 1	April 7	April 14	April 21	April 28
Record High	90°F	97°F	94°F	95°F	94°F
Average High	76°F	77°F	79°F	80°F	81°F
Average Low	54°F	56°F	57°F	59°F	61°F
Record Low	30°F	34°F	38°F	43°F	47°F
Sunrise	7:20 a.m.	7:13 a.m.	7:05 a.m.	6:57 a.m.	6:50 a.m.
Sunset	7:50 p.m.	7:53 p.m.	7:58 p.m.	8:02 p.m.	8:07 p.m.
Daylight	12 hr 30 min	12 hr 40 min	12 hr 53 min	13 hr 5 min	13 hr 16 min

Average Monthly Precipitation—3.25 inches

Spring Heralds

Nature has a way of letting us know when spring has arrived in the Hill Country of Central Texas. In addition to increasing temperatures, the awakening of birds, butterflies, and native plants are among the harbingers that mark the arrival of the season.

More than half of the birds recorded in Texas are migrants. Returning north in the spring to exploit the more productive temperate regions, they come in search of abundant food supplies, longer daylight hours, and less competition for nesting space. Texans have the advantage of being situated in the path of two "flyways" or principal routes used by North American birds—the Mississippi Flyway and the Central Flyway—and of the 338 species of North American birds listed as Neotropical migrants, 333 are documented for Texas.

Listen for the song of the Chuck-will's-widow (*Caprimulgus carolinensis*), which sounds just like its name, rising up from the canyons in the twilight and pre-dawn hours. Delight in the acrobatic flight of a Scissor-tailed Flycatcher (*Tyrannus forficatus*), a pearl gray and white bird with salmon-pink underwings and very long outer tail feathers, whose return coincides with the leafing out of the native Honey Mesquite (*Prosopis glandulosa* var. *glandulosa*) trees.

Marvel at the nest-building skills of the Cliff Swallows (*Petrochelidon pyrrhonota*), who zoom down to creek beds gathering mud to build colonies of gourd-shaped nests under our bridges and overpasses. And watch for the Western Kingbird (*Tyrannus verticalis*), a gray bird with a pale breast and yellow belly, whose raucous calls are heard in between bouts of insect-chasing from perches high in our neighborhood trees.

▲ *A male Scissor-tailed Flycatcher displaying its flowing tail and salmon-pink underwings.*

▶ *Inclined toward open habitats, the Western Kingbird chatters from a conspicuous perch.*

Aerial Acrobats

■ Other migrants returning to Central Texas at this time of year include the Barn Swallow (*Hirundo rustica*) and the Chimney Swift (*Chaetura pelagica*). Characterized by their swooping flights and aerial foraging for insects, both of these species spend much of their lives in the air. Barn Swallows are blue-black above with dark cinnamon throats, buffy breasts, and deeply forked tails. Their long, musical twitter is often heard while they hunt for insects under streetlamps in the early morning hours. Unlike Cliff Swallows that build gourd-like nests of mud in dense colonies, Barn Swallows build cuplike nests of mud under eaves and live in loose colonies. Chimney Swifts are swallow-like, but structurally distinct, and are often described as "flying cigars" with their dark plumage and sickle-shaped wings. Historically they nested in hollow trees, but readily adapted to masonry chimneys as the pioneers moved westward and cleared their natural habitat. Learn more about these adaptable swifts at www.chimneyswifts.org.

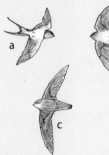

Cliff swallow nests, made of bits of dried mud, are usually found under rocky ledges, bridges, and overpasses.

Common swallows and swifts, as viewed from below (not to scale): Cliff Swallow (a), Barn Swallow (b), and Chimney Swift (c).

The sweet scents of early-blooming native plants catch our attention and the attention of many pollinating insects. Some of the most fragrant include the Texas Mountain Laurel (*Sophora secundiflora*), whose glossy, evergreen leaves form the perfect backdrop for huge clusters of deep purple to whitish flowers, up to 10 inches long, that smell like grape Kool-Aid. Or the less common Mexican Plum (*Prunus mexicana*), a small tree identified by its numerous and intensely fragrant white blossoms, which like the pink blossoms of the Mexican Buckeye (*Ungnadia speciosa*) and the Texas Redbud (*Cercis canadensis*

The fragrant white blossoms of the Mexican Plum are a harbinger of spring.

This Juniper Hairstreak butterfly, nectaring on a blooming Yaupon, is named for the threadlike tails on its hindwings.

var. *texensis*) and the yellow blossoms of the Elbowbush (*Forestiera pubescens*), appear on the tree before the leaves begin to emerge. Many of these native plants provide nectar for several species of bees, and are nectar and/or larval food sources for spectacular butterflies such as the Giant Swallowtail (*Papilio cresphontes*), Two-tailed Swallowtail (*Papilio multicaudata*), Great Purple Hairstreak (*Atlides halesus*), Juniper Hairstreak (*Callophrys gryneus*), Long-tailed Skipper (*Urbanus proteus*), and Henry's Elfin (*Callophrys henrici*).

Wildflowers begin to grace our fields and roadsides, starting with the famous Texas Bluebonnet (*Lupinus texensis*), intermingled with Indian Paintbrush (*Castilleja indivisa*), pink Evening Primrose (*Oenothera speciosa*),

The Indian Blanket, or Firewheel, is a native wildflower easily grown from seed.

Winecup (*Callirhoe involucrata*), and Indian Blanket or Firewheel (*Gaillardia pulchella*), to name a few. These swaths of multi-colored gems not only delight the eye and provide the perfect setting for those Easter family photos, but they are a key element of the Hill Country ecosystem, and should be protected and propagated for the visual enjoyment and habitat value they provide all living things.

This April, take the time to go outside and discover for yourself the distinctive essence of a Hill Country spring. As Lyndon Baines Johnson, one of our more famous Texans said, "The beauty of our land is a natural resource. Its preservation is linked to the inner prosperity of the human spirit." Celebrate it!

April

Wildflowers for Summer and Fall Blooms

EARLY SPRING—WARMING WEATHER—IS A GOOD TIME TO SOW SEEDS FOR SOME SUMMER AND FALL ANNUAL WILDFLOWERS.

COMMON NAME	BLOOM TIME
Prairie Agalinis (*Agalinis heterophylla*)	June–October
Partridge Pea (*Chamaecrista fasciculata*)	June–October
Goldenwave (*Coreopsis* sp.)	April–July
Eryngo (*Eryngium leavenworthii*)	July–September
Snow-on-the-Mountain (*Euphorbia marginata*)	August–October
Indian Blanket (*Gaillardia pulchella*)	May–August
Maximilian Sunflower* (*Helianthus maximiliani*) (*Spanish name is *mirasol*, meaning "looks at the sun")	August–October
Tahoka Daisy (*Machaeranthera tanacetifolia*)	May–October
Clammyweed (*Polanisia dodecandra*)	May–October
Tropical Sage (*Salvia coccinea*)	February–October

WHERE TO WATCH:

❖ Elbowbush, Texas Redbud, Mountain Laurel, and Mexican Plum can all be found blooming on hills and alongside trails near water, in places like Bull Creek Greenbelt, Stennis Tract, and McKinney Falls State Park.

❖ Western Kingbirds can be heard and seen calling from the tops of live oak trees in many suburban neighborhoods and shopping center parking lots, and Scissor-tailed Flycatchers are often found perched on power lines near open, grassy areas.

❖ Native wildflowers can be seen along many of Austin's roadways, but are best observed up-close at the Lady Bird Johnson Wildflower Center.

The Song of the Vireo

As a family, vireos are small to medium-sized birds that seem similar to warblers at first glance, apart from their heavier bill and generally dull-green plumage. In fact, the word *vireo* is Latin for "I am green." Most vireo species are migratory, and return to their breeding grounds in early spring. Of the 13 true vireo species that are present in the United States and Canada, none is more at risk than the Black-capped Vireo (*Vireo atricapilla*), which has been on the endangered species list since 1987. At 4½ inches long, it is the smallest vireo that occurs regularly in the United States, and ranges from only three counties in Oklahoma to Central and West Texas, and south to North and Central Mexico.

A handsome songbird, adult male Black-capped Vireos are olive green above and white below with faint yellow flanks and wing bars. A glossy black cap is broken by white spectacles that frame brownish-red irises, and the bill is black, sturdy, and slightly hooked at the tip. It takes two years for a male to reach full adult plumage. Females are similarly marked but a bit duller in color, and have a slate gray crown and greenish-yellow underparts.

Black-capped Vireos have the largest repertoire of song notes to draw from, about ten times larger than other vireos. The males are persistent singers, usually vocalizing in melodious phrases of two to four notes separated by one to three second pauses. They can also emit several calls, including a scolding *zhrree,* especially while vigorously defending their territory. Insectivores, they glean leaves, twigs, and branches, sometimes hanging upside down or hovering, as they feed on beetles and caterpillars.

Black-capped Vireos nest in brushy areas called "shinneries." Groups of shin oak, evergreen sumac, or other shrubs/small trees of appropriately low height and density are critical success factors for breeding, with the most important requirement being foliage that extends to ground level. Once trees begin to reach to full size, the vireos will look for other early succession sites in which to breed. Nests are an open, hanging cup, only 15–50 inches from the ground, and are made of leaves, grasses, plant fiber, and spider silk. Obscured from view by foliage, they are often decorated with items like lichens or bits of paper. The opening to the nest is usually narrower than the nest itself, but the nest is deep enough so that an adult bird can sit inside with only its bill and tail tip showing.

Both the male and female share the task of nest construction and incubation. After the three or four eggs that are laid have hatched, the female does most of the brooding while the male supplies most of the food. While breeding pairs are sometimes able to produce more than one clutch of eggs during the breeding season, the male cares for some or all of the fledglings, while the female re-nests, sometimes with another male.

The Black-capped Vireo is endangered due to multiple threats of brood

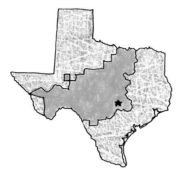

▲ Summer breeding range for the Black-capped Vireo in Central Texas.

▶ The female Black-capped Vireo shares incubation duties with the male.

▼ A good example of the low, shrubby vegetation preferred by nesting Black-capped Vireos.

parasitism by the Brown-headed Cowbird (*Molothrus ater*) as well as loss of suitable habitat through rapid urbanization, fire exclusion, livestock overgrazing, and excessive brush control. Female cowbirds may remove some of the host eggs from the nest and replace them with their own or lay their eggs with host eggs. Cowbird eggs hatch first and the quickly growing nestlings out-compete the smaller vireo nestlings for food and nest space. Cowbird trapping and habitat maintenance and creation through prescribed burning and mechanical manipulation are a high management priority in prime areas like the Balcones Canyonlands Preserve (BCP) System.

Vireo Viewing Stand

◼ Located near the northern boundary of the Balcones Canyonlands National Wildlife Refuge (BCNWR), the Shin Oak Observation deck is one of the easiest places to access Black-capped Vireo habitat and hear/see the bird itself. Open almost all year round, excluding a few weekends in the fall and for a brief period in the early spring when the vireos return, a short path to a large covered deck with built-in benches allows visitors within earshot and viewing of three to five vireo territories. It is the only regularly available public viewing area for vireos in the refuge, a 46,000 acre preserve managed by the U.S. Fish & Wildlife Service. Our other endangered bird, the Golden-cheeked Warbler, can be seen at the refuge's Warbler Vista and Sunset Deck, offering foot trails open every day from sunrise to sunset. Find out what you can explore at the refuge and when, by visiting www.fws .gov/southwest/refuges/texas/balcones.

The vireo viewing stand at the Shinoak Observation Deck.

* Visit the vireo viewing stand at the Shin Oak Observation Deck on the Balcones Canyonlands National Wildlife Refuge.
* Each year in late April, the Friends of Balcones Canyonlands National Wildlife Refuge hosts the Balcones Songbird Festival, which includes nature tours to view warblers and vireos.

Surprises After a Rain

Magical things happen when it rains in the Texas Hill Country! Historically, spring and fall generally bring the most amount of precipitation to our area, and the flora and fauna respond accordingly. Exotic-looking rain lilies pop up and bloom a few days after a good rain, but what you might not know is that there are two species of this delicate plant that are native to the Austin area.

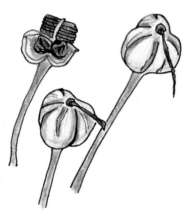

▲ *Rain lily seed pods.*

▶ *The solitary fall-blooming Evening Rain Lily.*

A group of spring-blooming Hill Country Rain Lilies.

Hill Country Rain Lily (*Cooperia pedunculata*), tends to have a main spring bloom season after significant rains occurring March through early August, although it can bloom sporadically over the rest of the growing season. These lilies begin to open slowly at dusk and are fully opened the next morning. An all-white bloom with three petals and three sepals, the flower is trumpet-shaped, roughly 2 inches across, and is at the top of a single unbranched blue-green stem about 5 to 9 inches high. The leaves are thin, long, and branch away from the stem at the base. The slightly fragrant bloom lasts only a day or two, turning from white to light pink as it fades. Often found in groups in

Fallouts

■ Each spring, millions of birds that wintered in Central America and South America migrate north to the Yucatan Peninsula and fly across the Gulf of Mexico in search of summer breeding territories. In early March, as conditions are favorable, they leave Mexico just after sunset. The trip is 600 miles and lasts 18 hours, so in good weather they can reach the Texas coast by the next day, with most of them flying inland by nightfall. Occasionally, from early March to mid-May, conditions exist where turbulent, strong north winds and rainfall trigger a phenomenon called a "fallout." Typically occurring when a fast-moving cold front crosses Texas and moves into the Gulf of Mexico during the middle of the day, it causes the migrating birds to slow down and rapidly lose their stored energy reserves. Forced to land and seek shelter, food, and rest, large, mixed flocks of birds can be found concentrated along the coast and inland as far north as Austin. This phenomenon highlights all the more reason for preservation of good-quality habitat to exist for the thousands of these birds grounded along the coast and up into Central Texas.

meadows, open woodlands, and even roadsides, these lilies can be grown easily from seeds or bulbs and combine well with groundcovers or plants that have naturally short foliage. They are native to Eastern and Southwestern Texas as well as adjacent Mexico, and have since spread east to Louisiana.

Evening Rain Lily (*Cooperia drummondii*), tends to have an overlapping but slightly later bloom season, occurring from late May through September, with the most frequent flowering in late summer and fall after a substantial rain. The solitary, fragrant, and ephemeral white flower is made up of six petals and tops a leafless, 12 inch stem. It too opens in the evening, and after two to four days the flower turns pink and withers. After it fades, the smooth, gray-green, grass-like leaves elongate. The bloom is quite similar to but slightly smaller than the Hill Country Rain Lily.

Originally native to Northern Mexico, the western two-thirds of Texas to New Mexico, and Southeastern Kansas and Louisiana, the Evening Rain Lily has expanded its range to Oklahoma, Arkansas, Mississippi, and Alabama. It gets its scientific species name from Thomas Drummond, a naturalist born in Scotland who arrived in Weslaco, Texas in 1833. He spent 21 months working the area between Galveston Island and the Edwards Plateau, focusing on plants and birds along the Brazos, Guadalupe, and Colorado rivers, and contributing extensively to natural history collections for museums and scientific institutions around the world.

The next time you see some of these elegant beauties gracing an open field or a grassy area on the side of a road, think of them as a treasured gift given to you by a recent rain and a reminder that the rains bring more than just rainbows.

WHERE TO WATCH:

❖ A few days after a rain, both types of rain lilies can usually be seen blooming intermingled among grasses along roadsides and in meadows throughout the Austin area.

Evening Chorus

From late winter into late spring, many of the night sounds you hear are not insects at all, but members of a wide-ranging group of cricket, tree, chorus, and chirping frogs. These frogs have adaptations that reveal their mostly arboreal lifestyle, such as forward-facing eyes for binocular-like vision, adhesive pads on their fingers and toes, and a fondness for eating insects. Often not seen due to their diminutive size, these frogs are commonly mistaken for insects, due to their ability to produce loud and varied mating calls. Known as

Green Tree Frog.

"advertisement calls," these calls are produced by the males to attract females and warn other rival males during the breeding season.

The Green Tree Frog (*Hyla cinerea*) is a common, 1 to 2 inch frog with a slender, bright green body, cream-colored belly, and white lips that extend into lateral stripes along the sides of its body. Found in the eastern third of our state, this frog walks rather than jumps when on the ground. It is nocturnal, and prefers wet areas such as swamps, edges of lakes, and stream sides. During its breeding season from March to October, the males start calling just before dark, and sound like groups of tiny ducks quacking. Females, which are slightly larger than the males and lack the wrinkled vocal pouch, lay their fertilized eggs enclosed in a jelly envelope attached to floating vegetation. Influenced by the weather, breeding often takes place during or after a rain.

At ½ to 1½ inches, Blanchard's Cricket Frog (*Acris crepitans blanchardi*) is found throughout most of the state, except for the Panhandle and West Texas.

A Blanchard's Cricket Frog has a signature triangular patch between the eyes that points down its back.

Gray to green-brown, this frog has a long rounded snout, dark bands behind its limbs, and a distinguishing triangular patch behind the eyes that points down its back. Diurnal and active all year, these frogs prefer shallow but permanent ponds with vegetation and full sun. Often seen basking during the daytime, they will jump quickly into the water or away when disturbed, and are capable of covering 6 feet in one leap! Although they are part of the tree frog family, they are much more terrestrial and are excellent swimmers. When chorusing, especially at night, the male's call sounds like clicking small rocks or pebbles together. Mating occurs in late spring, with the female laying one egg at a time on submerged vegetation.

Strecker's Chorus Frog (*Pseudacris streckeri*) is a less common 1 to 1½ inch nocturnal frog that inhabits moist, wooded canyons and rocky ravines in the eastern half of the state. Its color can vary from gray to brown to olive, with a thick, dark stripe through and a dark spot under each eye, with longitudinal

The Strecker's Chorus Frog is essentially nocturnal and is known to burrow to escape heat and drought conditions.

The seldom seen Cliff Chirping Frog is associated with rock piles, outcrops, and shady canyon ledges.

Amphibian Watch

Texas Amphibian Watch (www.tpwd.state.tx.us/amphibians) is part of Texas Nature Trackers, a collection of biological monitoring projects administered by Texas Parks & Wildlife and manned by trained volunteer citizen scientists. Amphibians, due to their two-stage lifecycle and water-permeable eggs and skin are early bio-indicators of habitat and water quality. This project collects long-term data to help understand what is happening to our amphibian populations.

spots on its back. Often, this frog can show a deep orange or yellow coloration around the groin. While it prefers loose soil where it can burrow to protect itself from predators, drought, and daytime heat, it is also a strong climber. Unlike many other frog species, this frog breeds from November to April or May, when you may hear a single male's call of one bell-like note, repeated rapidly, or a chorus of asynchronous calls from multiple individuals that sound like a squeaky wheel.

At ¾ to 1½ inches, the nocturnal Cliff Chirping Frog (*Syrrhophus marnockii*) is found in the cracks and crevices of limestone cliffs. Mostly green with brown mottling and dark crossbars on its hind limbs, this frog also has a proportionately large head and big eyes. It can run, leap, and hop, and its flattened body allows it to slip into cracks in the rocks to avoid predators. Sounding a bit like a shy cricket, the call of the Cliff Chirping Frog is a series of short, clear chirps and trills. While calls are made throughout the year, they are sharper and clearer when females are present. From February to December females may lay eggs as many as three times in moist leaf litter or soil, although peak breeding occurs in April and May.

When you're out at night from winter to late spring or early summer and near one of our natural areas, sit quietly and in no time you should be able to identify the unmistakable sounds of arboreal ardor.

WHERE TO WATCH:

❖ The Green Tree Frog, Strecker's Chorus Frog, and Cliff Chirping Frog are more often heard than seen, so listen for their distinctive calls near moist, rocky canyons, springs, and seeps like those found at Barton Creek and Bull Creek Greenbelts and Walnut Creek Metropolitan Park.

❖ More commonly seen, Blanchard's Cricket Frogs can be found at the shallow edges of more permanent water sources, like small ponds and creek drainages at places like Berry Springs, Mary Moore Searight Park, and Slaughter Creek Greenbelt.

❖ Join the Texas Amphibian Watch project and become a trained volunteer.

When perched, the brilliant blue upperside of the Great Purple Hairstreak is hidden and only reveals itself in flight.

CLIMATIC DATA FOR THE MONTH OF MAY IN AUSTIN.

	May 1	May 7	May 14	May 21	May 28
Record High	98°F	102°F	96°F	99°F	99°F
Average High	82°F	83°F	84°F	86°F	87°F
Average Low	62°F	63°F	65°F	67°F	68°F
Record Low	40°F	41°F	49°F	52°F	47°F
Sunrise	6:48 a.m.	6:43 a.m.	6:38 a.m.	6:34 a.m.	6:31 a.m.
Sunset	8:09 p.m.	8:13 p.m.	8:17 p.m.	8:22 p.m.	8:26 p.m.
Daylight	13 hr 21 min	13 hr 30 min	13 hr 40 min	13 hr 48 min	13 hr 55 min

Average Monthly Precipitation—4.33 inches

Wildscaping with Natives

Are you interested in attracting beautiful song birds, jewel-like butterflies, and other interesting wildlife to your yard? Wildscaping, or gardening for wildlife, has many wonderful benefits. Aside from restoring the natural habitat and nurturing wildlife all year long, wildscaping can provide a unique education for the whole family, by expanding your gardening knowledge and enjoyment of nature. It can give you a more attractive, interesting yard—a peaceful, restful sanctuary—that benefits both the environment and your

The authors' wildscaped yard includes a moving water feature surrounded by native plants.

pocketbook by reducing chemical use, conserving water, and improving the air, water, and soil quality in your neighborhood.

As outlined by the National Wildlife Federation, a good wildlife garden contains all of the following elements: food, water, cover, and places to raise young. While you can certainly supplement food by putting out seed in bird feeders, the easiest way to provide it is by planting native plants. Once established, they require little care and offer a much more natural and seasonal variety of seeds, nectar, fruits, and berries. Water can be made available through a simple bird bath or a more complex water feature or pond. The sound of dripping or moving water, achieved by using a mister or a pump, is a great attractor for wildlife. And lastly, in order for wildlife to feel safe, they need to have places to hide and longer-term shelters to raise their young. Cover can be provided in many forms, from planting thick shrubs to putting up birdhouses and nesting boxes and creating log, brush, or rock piles.

As part of the city government's commitment to declare Austin a community wildlife habitat, now is the time to join the wildscaping trend and start making the transition to native plants. How you manage your garden or landscape can have an effect on the overall health of the soil, air, water and habitat for native wildlife as well as our human community. Help conserve and

Native, colorful blooming plants require little water and attract butterflies and other beneficial insects.

A Gray Hairstreak (Strymon melinus) *sips nectar through a slit at the base of an Esperanza* (Tecoma stans) *blossom created by a bee.*

Four key elements of a good wildlife habitat: food (a), water (b), places to raise young (c), and cover (d).

improve the quality of these resources by using sustainable gardening practices such as mulching and composting, reducing or eliminating lawn areas, xeriscaping (planting native, drought-tolerant plants), installing rain barrels, and removing invasive plants and restoring native ones.

The U.S. government defines an invasive plant species as one "that is not native to the ecosystem under consideration and whose introduction is likely to cause economic or environmental harm or harm to human health." These species grow outside desired boundaries, out-competing native species, and spread by seeds, berries, spores, runners, rhizomes, and stems. Some can be easily transported long distances, and every year millions of our tax dollars are spent trying to eradicate them.

Many of these plants have already invaded our preserves and greenbelts in Austin, originating in our landscapes, escaping cultivation and spreading into the wild. Invasive species may grow faster, taller, or wider and shade out native species. Many stay green later into the season or leaf out earlier, giving them an advantage over natives. They can change the vertical and horizontal structure of ecosystems, alter hydrology, and disrupt nutrient cycles, all of which can have devastating effects on native plants and animals.

Although invasive exotics may offer birds fruit, squirrels nuts, and hummingbirds and butterflies nectar, they do not provide the entire range of seasonal habitat benefits that an appropriate locally native species will provide. If we want not only to satisfy our desires to attract wildlife, but also to restore the critical, often unseen, small pieces in our ecosystems, we need to bring back our locally native plants. These plants meet the food and cover needs of all wildlife species: bees, wasps, butterflies, grasshoppers, bugs, beetles, spiders, and thousands of others that sustain and support food webs which songbirds, salamanders, bats, toads, and box turtles more visibly demonstrate.

Aside from attracting a diversity of wildlife, the use of native plants minimizes the impact our landscapes have on the natural environment around us. They reduce water consumption, eliminate the need for chemical fertilizers and pesticides, and limit the competition from invasive exotics. This results in a much healthier habitat—water, soil, and air—for humans and animals alike, and is less costly, too. Invite wildlife to put on a show in your yard by replacing some of the invasives in your landscape, and encourage your neighbors to do the same.

▲ *A Crimson Patch* (Chlosyne janais) *butterfly deposits her eggs on the underside of a Flame Acanthus* (Anisacanthus quadrifidus *var.* wrightii) *leaf.*

◄ *Rock Rose or Pavonia flowers open in early morning and are gone by mid-afternoon.*

A Pipevine Swallowtail (Battus philenor) nectaring on Indian Blanket flower.

While the intricate blooms of passionvines appeal to humans, the leaves are the preferred larval foodplant for several species of butterflies.

The Two-tailed Swallowtail (Papilio multicaudata) is the largest of all western butterflies.

A LIST OF INVASIVE PLANTS COMMON THROUGHOUT AUSTIN, AND SOME NATIVE AND ADAPTED ALTERNATIVES.

Invasive Plant(s)	Some Native & Adapted Alternative(s)
Bamboo	Wax Myrtle (*Morella cerifera*) Yaupon Holly (*Ilex vomitoria*) Bamboo Muhly (*Muhlenbergia dumosa*)
Chinaberry	Chinquapin Oak *(Quercus muehlenbergii)* Texas Red Oak *(Quercus buckleyi)*
Chinese Tallow Tree	Bigtooth Maple (*Acer grandidentatum*) Lacey Oak (*Quercus laceyi*)
Elephant Ear	Arrowhead (*Sagittaria latifolia*) Crinum Lily (*Crinum americanum*) Tuckahoe (*Peltandra virginica*) Pigeonberry (*Rivina humilis*) Frogfuit (*Phyla nodiflora*) Horseherb (*Calyptocarpus vialis*)
Giant Cane	Roughleaf Dogwood (*Cornus drummondii*) Yaupon Holly (*Ilex vomitoria*)
Japanese Honeysuckle	Coral Honeysuckle (*Lonicera sempervirens*) Passion Vine (*Passiflora foetida* or *P. incarnata* or *P. lutea* or *P. tenuiloba*) Rock Rose (*Pavonia lasiopetala*)
Holly Fern	River Fern (*Thelypteris kunthii*)
Kudzu, English Ivy, Vinca	Virginia Creeper (*Parthenocissus quinquefolia*) Trumpet Vine (*Campsis radicans*) Coral Vine (*Antigonon leptopus*)
Ligustrum (all species) or Common Privet	Evergreen Sumac (*Rhus virens*) Barbados Cherry (*Malpighia glabra*) Yaupon Holly (*Ilex vomitoria*) Possumhaw Holly (*Ilex decidua*) Texas Sage (*Leucophyllum frutescens*) Cherry Laurel (*Prunus caroliniana*)
Mimosa	Desert Willow (*Chilopsis linearis*) Texas Redbud (*Cercis canadensis* var. *texensis*) Elbowbush (*Forestiera pubescens*)
Nandina or Heavenly Bamboo	Texas Lantana (*Lantana urticoides*) Trailing Lantana (*Lantana montevidensis*) Bush Germander (*Teucrium fruticans*) Texas Sage (*Leucophyllum frutescens*)
Paper or White Mulberry	Red Mulberry (*Morus rubra*) Texas Persimmon (*Diospyros texana*) Possumhaw Holly (*Ilex decidua*) Cherry Laurel (*Prunus caroliniana*)
Pyracantha	Yaupon Holly (*Ilex vomitoria*) Possumhaw Holly (*Ilex decidua*) Evergreen Sumac (*Rhus virens*)

▶

May

Invasive Plant(s)	Some Native & Adapted Alternative(s)
Red-tipped or Chinese Photinia	Evergreen Sumac (*Rhus virens*) Carolina Buckthorn (*Frangula caroliniana*) Yaupon Holly (*Ilex vomitoria*)
Russian Olive	Texas Persimmon (*Diospyros texana*)
St. Augustine Grass	Buffalo Grass (*Bouteloua dactyloides*) (or better yet, reduce or completely eliminate turf!)
Tamarisk or Salt Cedar	Bald Cypress (*Taxodium distichum*) Arizona Cypress (*Cupressus arizonica*)
Tree of Heaven	Chinquapin Oak (*Quercus muehlenbergii*) Lacey Oak (*Quercus laceyi*)
Vitex or Chastetree	Texas Pistachio (*Pistacia mexicana*) Mexican Buckeye (*Ungnadia speciosa*)
Wisteria	Passion Vine (*Passiflora foetida* or *P. incarnata* or *P. lutea* or *P. tenuiloba*) Trumpet Vine (*Campsis radicans*)

Native Plant Society of Texas

■ Promoting the conservation, research, and use of native plants and plant habitats of Texas is the Native Plant Society of Texas (NPSOT). The Austin chapter (www.npsot.org/Austin) has informative monthly meetings (normally held at Wild Basin Preserve off Loop 360), local events, and access to regional plant experts. Online plant database and checklists are excellent references.

WHERE TO WATCH:

❖ While the premiere showcase for native plant gardens is the Lady Bird Johnson Wildflower Center, other public places to visit include the gardens at Austin City Hall, Texas Parks & Wildlife Headquarters, McKinney Roughs, and the native plant section of Zilker Gardens.

❖ Buy a copy of Kelly Conrad Bender's book, *Texas Wildscapes: Gardening for Wildlife,* published by Texas A&M University Press, to help you plan your own personal wildscape.

Filter Feeders

What makes no sound and cannot see? Often lives for decades, but seldom moves from a secure spot? Causing a stir, making us ponder their future as well as our own? The answer to this riddle is freshwater mussels! Nearly 300 species of native freshwater mussels (also called unionids) live in the United States, with more than 50 species found in Texas. Yet nearly 70 percent of the known species are extinct, endangered, or in need of special protection, largely due to the changes that have occurred in their ecosystem in the last 200 years.

Living buried in the sand and gravel at the bottom of rivers and streams, with a few adapted to the quiet waters of lakes and ponds, freshwater mussels are filter feeders. They draw their food to them by siphoning water into their shells, using their gills to filter out algae and small particles from the water, and to take in oxygen. Although freshwater mussels have a muscular "foot," they don't move very much but use this foot to burrow into the mud or to provide limited travel if disturbed by droughts or floods.

Freshwater mussels are protected from predators by a hard, calcium-based shell consisting of two halves joined by a hinge. Thin-shelled species live on average 4 to 10 years, whereas thick-shelled species can live 20 to 40 years or more. With colorful common names including terms like floater, pocketbook, fatmucket, pimpleback, pistol grip, and washboard, Texas unionids were often named after items that resembled the shapes of their shells, by those who harvested them for their pearls and for use in the shell-button industry. Fifteen species of Texas freshwater mussels are now on the state threatened list, which means they are protected and cannot be collected or killed. Those found in the Colorado River system in Central Texas include the False Spike (*Quadrula mitchelli*), Smooth Pimpleback (*Quadrula houstonensis*), Texas Fatmucket (*Lampsilis bracteata*), Texas Fawnsfoot (*Truncilla macrodon*), and the Texas Pimpleback (*Quadrula petrina*).

In addition to their unusual common names, these bivalves also have a very unusual reproductive cycle. First, eggs held inside the female

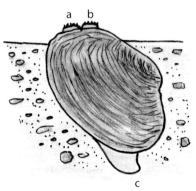

Basic freshwater mussel anatomy: incurrent siphon (a), excurrent siphon (b), and foot (c).

▲ The Smooth Pimpleback, also called the Houston or Southern Pimpleback, occurs in mixed mud, sand, and fine gravel.

▲ The Texas Fatmucket is found in sand, mud, and gravel in moderately flowing waters.

▼ The Texas Fawnsfoot occurs in the Colorado River drainage.

▼ The Texas Pimpleback is found in mud and gravel in shallow, slow-flowing waters.

need to be fertilized by sperm released into the water from a nearby male. The resulting young mussels, or "glochidia," are in turn released by the female and temporarily attach themselves to a fish's fins or gills. This sounds like tricky business, and it is! Some female mussels have evolved to attract certain species of host fish by using insect, worm, and fish-shaped lures—tissue-based exten-

Mussel Watch

■ Texas Mussel Watch (www
.tpwd.state.tx.us/learning/texas_
nature_trackers/mussel/) is part
of Texas Nature Trackers, a collection of biological monitoring
projects administered by Texas
Parks & Wildlife and manned by
trained volunteer citizen scientists. No special equipment is
needed to monitor for freshwater
mussels, and volunteers can help
determine the distribution and
relative abundance of these species, and monitor for any changes.

sions of their bodies—that have developed to bring the fish in close enough
for the dispersed glochidia to attach.
During this parasitic stage, the glochidia
grow into tiny mussels and within a few
weeks drop from the fish and down to
the river bottom or stream bed to mature and continue the cycle.

Sadly, there are many reasons for the
decline of freshwater mussel populations
in Texas, and most of them are human-
made. Changes in the natural flow of
rivers and streams due to dams and lake
construction, increased deposition of silt
due to runoff caused by the clearing of
indigenous vegetation, introduction of
aquatic contaminants and exotic plant species, and the lack of native fish hosts
are a few of those reasons contributing to the decline. Freshwater mussels are
an important indicator of the vitality of our aquatic ecosystems. Healthy populations would reflect more pure, clean water for humans as well as many other
aquatic plants and animals.

WHERE TO WATCH:

❖ Because most freshwater mussel species are rare, threatened, or endangered, you can best see them by joining the Texas Mussel Watch project and
becoming a trained volunteer.

Pollinators: A Flower's Best Friend

With their beautiful colors, interesting shapes, and enticing scents, the
main purpose of flowers is to attract pollinators and ensure the reproduction
of the flowering plant. A pollinator is the biotic agent that moves pollen from
the male parts of a flower (anthers) to the female parts of a flower (stigma) to
accomplish fertilization. Why is this so important? Aside from the propagation of native plant species, over 150 grain and fruit food crops depend on this
process—without it we would have no almonds, coffee, apples, or chocolate!

Although some birds, bats, and small mammals (and even a lizard in some

Botanical parts of a generalized flower. The pistil is made up of the stigma (a), style (b), and ovary (c). The stamen is the anther (d) and the filament (e). Petals (f) and sepals (g) are often the most recognizable parts of a flower.

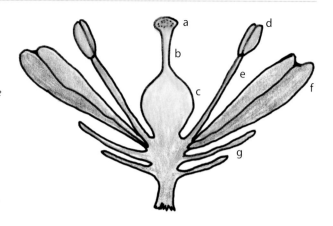

A native Halictid sweat bee pollinating a Brown-eyed Susan (Rudbeckia hirta) bloom.

parts of the world) act as pollinators, the vast majority of this job is done by flying insects. The most recognized pollinators are various species of bees, which are clearly adapted to pollination. Their surface is fuzzy and carries an electrostatic charge, and both of these features help pollen grains adhere to their bodies. Bees often also have structures on their abdomen or legs that have evolved to carry pollen. Honey bees gather both nectar and pollen, using them to nurture their young, while transferring pollen between flowers as they are working.

Hummingbirds act as pollinators for various species of deep-throated flowers, a perfect example of how plants fall into different categories called "pollination syndromes." Each syndrome is defined by a collection of characteristics that attract a certain type of pollinator. Hummingbirds love to visit red flowers

Even non-native European honeybees can act as pollinators.

with long narrow tubes and lots of nectar, but are not as strongly attracted to wide flowers with little nectar and copious amounts of pollen. Butterfly-pollinated flowers tend to be showy, pink or lavender in color, frequently have a good landing area, and are usually scented. Among the more important moth pollinators are the hawk moths, whose behavior is similar to hummingbirds except that they are nocturnal or crepuscular (active at dawn and dusk). As such, moth-pollinated flowers tend to be white, night-opening, with large blooms that produce a strong, sweet scent in the evening or early morning.

Today, there is alarming evidence that the pollinator population is in decline, threatened by habitat loss, degradation, and fragmentation. Pollinator visitation declines when native pollination syndromes are modified by planting non-native and unfamiliar plant species in our yards and public places. This helps to explain why it is important to the overall health of an ecosystem not to break the natural lifecycle and interrelationships of highly-evolved, coexisting native species by introducing or replacing them with non-native ones.

Thanks to the wonderful work of bees, butterflies, birds, and other animal pollinators, flowering plants are able to reproduce and bear fruit, providing many of the foods we eat, the plant materials we and other organisms use, and the natural beauty we see around us. If you are interested in doing your part to create a pollinator-friendly habitat, plan to use a variety of native plants that bloom from spring to fall, eliminate the use of chemical pesticides, include larval host plants to encourage caterpillars, and construct bee condos or human-made nesting blocks. Encouraging pollinators to your garden can "bee" a project the whole family can enjoy!

A female Ruby-throated Hummingbird with a pollen-covered crown.

Hawk moths, such as this Tersa Sphinx (Xylophanes tersa), commonly visit flowers at dusk.

This Datura, or Jimson-weed, blooms at night and is pollinated by moths.

WHERE TO WATCH:

❖ To observe and learn about native bees, visit the Austin Community Landfill Bee Garden at 9900 Giles Lane, which is managed by Texas Bee Watchers (www.beewatchers.com).

❖ Visit native plant gardens such as the Butterfly Garden at Zilker Gardens or The Natural Gardener during the day to look for hummingbirds and around dusk to find pollinating moths.

❖ Each year around Mother's Day weekend, the Lady Bird Johnson Wildflower Center conducts "Gardens On Tour," a great way to see native plant gardens throughout Austin.

The Lure and Lore of Lizards

Various beliefs, myths, and legends have been inspired by the behavioral patterns of lizards. In ancient Egypt and Greece the lizard represented divine wisdom and good fortune, in Roman mythology their hibernation symbolized death and resurrection, and in Australia the aboriginal people believed that the sky would fall if you killed one. Although few people hold to these beliefs today, lizards continue to fascinate us. Central Texas is home to several species of lizards, geckos, anoles, skinks, and whiptails, and those most likely (and interesting) to be seen are the Texas Spiny Lizard (*Sceloporus olivaceus*), the Green or Carolina Anole (*Anolis carolinensis*), and the Texas Alligator Lizard (*Gerrhonotus infernalis*).

Primarily arboreal but preferring basking surfaces such as fence posts and rock walls, the Texas Spiny Lizard is quite common in all but the eastern and western thirds of Texas. A large spiny lizard up to 11 inches long, it is grayish to olive brown with up to nine dark wavy bars spaced along its back, which gives it a very scaly appearance. Males have a narrow bright blue patch on each side of the belly, and while the females lack this coloration, they are slightly larger and paler than the males. An ambush predator, they feed on a variety of insects found on the ground in open areas or up in trees in wooded areas. Breeding occurs in the spring and summer, and mature females may lay several egg clutches per year.

Ranging from bright green to dark brown, the Green Anole possesses the ability to change color due to temperature and light. A small lizard, it has a pale colored underbelly, long claws, and a thin tail. The males have what is called a "dewlap," a bright pink flap of skin that can be extended and retracted for pur-

Texas Spiny Lizards are fast-moving and agile, rapidly ascending trees when frightened.

poses of intimidating rivals and attracting females during the mating season. These anoles are arboreal, spending most of their time in trees, shrubs, and vines, feeding on insects and spiders. Males will aggressively defend their small territories, starting with extending their dewlap, bobbing their head, performing pushups, and ultimately ending in a chase or a wrestling match. All this posturing and patrolling can make the males much easier targets for predators, however, and they tend to have higher mortality rates than the much more discreet females. If it is late spring and the right to mate is at stake, the winner will once again employ headbobbing and dewlap extension to entice the female, who lays a single, soft-shelled egg among the leaf litter.

Coming in at an impressive 10 to 24 inches long, the Texas Alligator Lizard is a stiff lizard with large, plate-like scales and a long, somewhat prehensile tail. It is the largest lizard in Texas and one of the largest alligator lizards in the world. Varying from ruddy yellow to reddish brown, it has dark crosshatching on its back with a lighter head and small, weak legs that are unmarked. Found on rocky hillsides, it has slow, calculated moves, feeding on insects, spiders, and small invertebrates. When alarmed, it may inflate itself in defense—and like other lizards even lose its tail to distract a potential predator—but more

The Green Anole is Texas' only anole with the ability to change color.

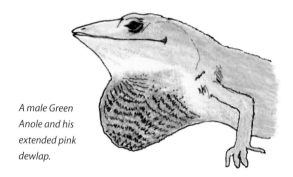

A male Green Anole and his extended pink dewlap.

typically it will fold in its legs and slither away like a snake. Unlike many other lizards, breeding can occur year-round, and multiple clutches of eggs can be laid. Females often stay near the nest site to protect it, but once the young hatch they receive no parental care.

Lizards have been around for 100 million years longer than humans, and descended from the same family tree that gave rise to the dinosaurs. The next time you're lucky enough to have one cross your path, show it some well-deserved respect.

Although common, the Texas Alligator Lizard is secretive and seldom seen.

Horny Toad

■ Commonly called a "horny toad," the Texas Horned Lizard (*Phryno-soma cornutum*) is a fierce-looking, flat-bodied lizard. Its head has numerous spines, the largest being two central horns on the middle of the head. With two rows of fringed scales along either side of its body, it is the only species of horned lizard to have dark brown stripes across the top of the head and radiating down from each eye. Once common throughout Texas, populations declined in the 1950s and 1960s due to pesticide use. Now found mainly in the western third of the state, it is listed as an endangered species. You can help by joining the Texas Horned Lizard Watch at www.tpwd.state.tx.us/hornedlizards.

WHERE TO WATCH:

❖ Commonly seen in wild places as well as suburban yards, look for lizards basking themselves on rocks, tree trunks, and other warm, sunny surfaces.

The beautiful Scarlet Leatherflower (Clematis texensis) is a specialty of the Edwards Plateau.

CLIMATIC DATA FOR THE MONTH OF JUNE IN AUSTIN

	June 1	June 7	June 14	June 21	June 28
Record High	100°F	100°F	108°F	106°F	104°F
Average High	88°F	89°F	91°F	92°F	93°F
Average Low	69°F	70°F	71°F	72°F	73°F
Record Low	55°F	60°F	57°F	60°F	63°F
Sunrise	6:30 a.m.	6:29 a.m.	6:29 a.m.	6:30 a.m.	6:32 a.m.
Sunset	8:28 p.m.	8:31 p.m.	8:34 p.m.	8:36 p.m.	8:37 p.m.
Daylight	13 hr 58 min	14 hr 2 min	14 hr 5 min	14 hr 6 min	14 hr 5 min

Average Monthly Precipitation—3.08 inches

June

Webs of Intrigue

Spending summer days in the fields, woods, and even our own suburban gardens can yield many interesting sights, but few are more curious than that of the spider web. Formed out of protein-rich silk extruded from a spider's spinnerets (or silk-producing organs located at their abdomens), webs can take many forms, including spiral orbs, tangles, funnels, tubes, sheets, domes, and tents. While most spiders can use both sticky and fluffy silk to construct a web, they can also position the web horizontally or vertically or at any angle in between, depending on its specific purpose.

Web construction is a unique and delicate process, with the spider using its own body for measurements. Starting with the most difficult part, the first thread, spiders use the wind (and a bit of luck) to carry it to an adhesive surface. Once caught, the spider will carefully walk over the thread while strengthening it with another thread, repeating this action until this primary thread is strong enough to support the finished web. Step two involves the process of making many radials, making sure that the distance between each radial is small enough to cross. Ergonomically speaking, this means that the number of radials in a web depends directly on the size of the spider and helps to determine the final size of the web.

Once the radials are complete, the spider will fortify the center of the web with several circular threads, and move outward, continu-

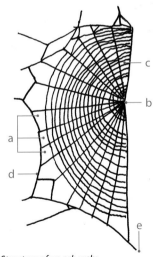

Structure of an orb web:
*radius (a), hub (b), sticky spiral (c),
frame (d), and anchor (e).*

ing a spiral of non-sticky, evenly-spaced threads made so the spider can easily move around its own web. Then, beginning from the outside edge and moving toward the center, it adds sticky spiral threads by utilizing the radials and non-sticky spirals as guidelines. Once again using its body as a measuring device, the spaces between each of the sticky spirals is directly proportional to the distance from the tips of its back legs to its spinnerets. After the sticky spirals are complete, the spider consumes the non-sticky spirals as they are no longer needed, chews off the initial center spiral threads and sits and waits for prey.

Webs are literally extensions of a spider's ability to feel, allowing them to catch their prey without having to expend the energy to run it down. Some spiders will decorate their webs with loose, irregular tangles of silk to disorient and knock down flying insects and to warn birds and other flying predators of the presence of the web. Constructing a web is energetically costly for a spider due to the large amount of protein required, so broken webs, especially if they are still structurally sound, are almost always repaired. It is not uncommon,

A Giant Lichen Orbweaver (Araneus bicentenarius) *spins a new web.*

Morning dew glistens like diamonds strung along the threads of a silken web.

Types of Spider Webs

■ The most common type of spider web is an orb web, which looks like a typical wheel with spokes. Tangled spider webs consist of a shapeless jumble of threads, usually attached to a corner of a window or a ceiling. Cobwebs are tangled webs that have collected dust and dirt. Sheet webs are flat sheets of silk often formed between blades of grass or branches of shrubs and trees. Over them, you will often find a net of crisscrossed threads, which when hit by an insect, cause it to fall to the sticky sheet below. Spiders that make these kinds of webs hang down beneath them, and quickly pull a trapped insect through the web, later repairing the damaged section. Funnel webs are large, flat, horizontal webs made of non-sticky silk with a funnel at one end. Constructed in grassy areas, the funnel web is open at both ends so the spider can escape if necessary. Feeling the vibration in the web from prey, the spider dashes out, bites the insect, and carries it back into the funnel.

however, for spiders to eat their own web daily to recoup some of the energy used in spinning and recycle the protein by spinning a new web. Normally, a spider's web will remain in one location for the entire summer, but spiders can change locations usually early in the season, if they find a place with better protection or better hunting.

Commonly, webs are about twenty times larger than the spider building it. Rich in vitamin K, which can be effective in clotting blood, spider webs were used several hundred years ago as gauze pads to stop an injured person's bleeding. Today, we know that the tensile strength of spider silk is greater than the same weight of steel and has a much improved elasticity. Research into its microstructure is being performed for potential and surprising applications such as bullet-proof vests and artificial tendons.

The next time you are out in your garden in the early morning hours and you come across a delicate spider web glistening with drops of dew like strings of tiny diamonds, appreciate what you are seeing for its natural beauty, strength, and purpose.

WHERE TO WATCH:

❖ Spider webs can commonly be found in suburban yards and gardens, and often stretched across trails in our area parks, greenbelts, and preserves.

❖ Don't forget to search low to the ground, because many spiders spin their webs among blades of grass.

In the Water and On the Land

Many people are surprised to learn that the popular distinction between frogs and toads is artificial, because toads are actually a particular group of frogs. When using common names, the term "frog" generally refers to species that have smooth and/or moist skins and are aquatic or semi-aquatic, and the term "toad" usually refers to species that have dry, warty skin and are largely terrestrial. Frogs and toads are amphibians which means they change from a juvenile, water-breathing form to an adult, air-breathing form as they mature.

Of the nine species of toads in Texas, all have dry, warty skin, and obvious parotoids or shoulder glands. These glands secrete a toxin that can vary (if you are the predator) from simply distasteful to potentially lethal. Toads lay their eggs in long strings in the water, as opposed to clumps on vegetation like most frogs. To mate, the smaller male embraces the larger female by clasping her from behind, underneath her forelimbs.

Widespread in the southeastern part of Texas is the Gulf Coast Toad (*Bufo valliceps valliceps*). Since it is not as well-adapted to the dry areas like some toad species, this toad is often found near water, whether it be a natural feature or where irrigation is frequently used. With females measuring up to 5 inches in length (not including their legs), this is one of the largest common toads in our area. Yellowish- or reddish-brown to rich brown, the Gulf Coast Toad's skin may also show highlights of orange, gold, or white. This toad is best identified by its extensive cranial ridge, a crest that runs from its nose over and past each eye to the back of its head, with a branch that wraps around the back side of each eye.

Active from dusk until well after

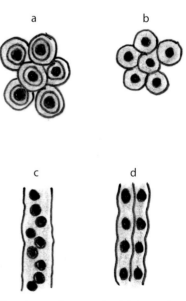

Frogs lay eggs in masses, toads in long strings: Rio Grande Leopard Frog (a), Northern Cricket Frog (b), Gulf Coast Toad (c, d).

Seasonal rains initiate breeding of Gulf Coast Toads.

nightfall, the males call from the edge or near the edge of the water with a short and low but loud trill that is repeated every few seconds. Like most other toads in Texas, the female Gulf Coast Toad usually lays her many thousands of eggs in long double strings from March to late summer, with breeding triggered by rains. In drier periods, these toads can be seen under street lamps and porch lights, searching for insects before returning to the same hiding spot to wait out the day.

Abundant near water, the Rio Grande Leopard Frog (*Rana berlandieri*) is one of the most commonly seen frogs in Central Texas. During wet periods, it is primarily diurnal (active during the day) whereas during a drought it is mostly nocturnal (active at night). Like most leopard frogs, this species has a smooth, sandy-tan to greenish-beige skin, with darker olive oval or rounded spots and light-colored ridges down either side of the back. It occurs through-out Central and West Texas, north to New Mexico, and south to Central Mexico, where it is also known as the Mexican Leopard Frog.

Like all frogs, this frog has a large, circular spot behind each eye, called a tympanic membrane or eardrum. Located on the sides of the head, they are typically larger in males than in females, and allow the frogs to locate one

The Rio Grande Leopard Frog is one of the most abundant frogs in our area.

Bufotoxins

■ The parotoid glands on common toads of the genus *Bufo* produce hallucinogens called bufotoxins. Often referred to as a toad's venom, these white, foamy neurotoxins are secreted to deter predators and may even kill them. While they look like warts, parotoid glands are normal, healthy parts of the animals that bear them. Their similarity in appearance to warts explains the old wives' tale that warts are caused by touching or handling toads.

another through vocalizations. In Central Texas, calls resembling a short, rapidly pulsed snore, interspersed with chuckling notes, are most frequently heard in late winter or early spring.

WHERE TO WATCH:

❖ Find Gulf Coast Toads in suburban yards (especially after rains or recent watering) and under streetlamps and porch lights in drier periods, hunting for insects.

❖ Rio Grande Leopard Frogs prefer more permanent water sources like ponds, lakes, and streams, and can also be attracted to suburban yards that provide water features.

❖ Join the Texas Amphibian Watch project and become a trained volunteer.

Signature Plants

As previously described, the Hill Country of Central Texas is defined as an environmental ecoregion, which means it contains a certain set of plants and animals whose presence indicates specific conditions such as temperature range, rainfall, food supply, and physical characteristics of the land. This set of species, called indicator or signature species, can be among the most sensitive in a region, acting as an early warning of changing conditions to monitoring biologists. Many of the signature plant species found on the Edwards Plateau are common, but several are quite rare.

Found only in five Texas counties (Blanco, Comal, Hayes, Kendall, and Travis), Canyon Mock Orange (*Philadelphus ernestii*) is a rare low shrub with small glossy green leaves and fragrant white blossoms. It grows near springs, among boulders and on bluffs in shady, moist canyons. Endemic to the Hill Country, this plant is almost identical to a more common but still uncommon species called Texas Mock Orange (*Philadelphus texensis*), which naturally occurs in Bandera, Edwards, Real, and Uvalde counties. Aside from slight geographic differences in location, the key to properly identifying each species lies in the hairs that cover the lower leaf surface—Canyon Mock Orange has only short straight hairs and Texas Mock Orange has a mix of short straight hairs and long tangled hairs. Listed as a state species of concern due to its declining numbers, Canyon Mock Orange is in need of environmental protection.

One of the most beautiful and uncommon shrubs found only on the Edwards Plateau is the Sycamoreleaf Snowbell (*Styrax platanifolius*). A sprawling, irregular, deciduous shrub, it grows on or under steep bluffs near creeks, offering showy white bell-shaped flowers in the spring and large green leaves with angular projections in the summer, turning to bright yellow in the fall. As a larval host plant, its leaves offer food for the caterpillars of Eastern Tiger Swallowtail (*Papilio glaucus*) butterflies. Several protection efforts by concerned citizens and botanists to propagate this plant are occurring on private lands.

Once scattered throughout Central Texas, the Bracted Twist-flower (*Streptanthus bracteatus*) is now a rare plant, likely due to the combined effect

The white flowers of the Canyon Mock Orange have a pleasant fragrance.

A blooming Sycamoreleaf Snowbell.

of picking by humans and overgrazing by livestock. Found on rocky, wooded slopes it grows 2–4 feet tall, with a base of long, lobed green leaves that become shorter and more rounded as they travel up the stem. Striking violet-purple multi-flower spikes 4–10 inches tall grace the plant in late spring, with each individual flower having a small bract or leaf at its base.

Climbing on shrubs and small trees and found in a variety of environments, the uncommon Bracted Passionflower Vine (*Passiflora affinis*) is yet another native jewel of the Hill Country. While its pale yellow-green flowers are small at only one inch across, they exhibit the typical intricacy of passionflower structure. Smooth, deeply lobed green leaves provide food to Zebra Longwing (*Heliconius charithonia*) and Gulf Fritillary (*Agraulis vanillae*) caterpillars, but also frequently sport tiny yellow spots, presumably to mimic butterfly eggs and discourage excessive egg laying that could lead to caterpillar-induced defoliation.

A colorful group of native orchids called *Hexalectris* are found mainly in the mountains of Northern Mexico, West Texas, and here in the Edwards Plateau and Blacklands Prairie regions of Texas. The name literally means "six cock's combs," referring to the six prominent ridges that were thought to run down the length of the flower's lower lip. But despite this name, most flowers have five or seven ridges. These orchids are micro-heterotrophic, which describes a plant that gets some or all of its food from parasitism on fungi rather than from photosynthesis. Most *Hexalectris* orchids have only been discovered and studied in the last fifty years. They depend heavily on an extremely delicate balance of environmental factors, which makes them impossible to transplant from the wild.

In the Austin area, April through August is the best time to spot the Spiked Crested Coralroot (*Hexalectris spicata* var. *spicata*). An uncommon orchid, it is most often found in the leaf litter on the wooded limestone hillsides and canyon slopes in oak-juniper woodland habitats of the Edwards Plateau. Also called Cock's Comb or Brunetta, the blooms of this coralroot grow on a tall, leafless, fleshy-pink stalk. Each bloom has creamy yellow petals and sepals striped with brownish-purple, and the central white lip is adorned with five to seven wavy crests of deep, royal purple. Recently, the first record of the Giant or Largeflower Crested Coralroot (*Hexalectris grandiflora*) was discovered in the Balcones Canyonlands Preserve in Travis County. Previously thought only to grow in the Davis and Chisos Mountains of West Texas, the bright pink, leafless stalk of this species grows from 10 to 24 inches tall. Along the stalk, vivid pink flowers bloom with a white mark in the center of an elaborately shaped, three-lobed lip. This coralroot also flourishes in our oak-juniper woodlands, and is thought to bloom from June to September. Other common names for this beautiful wild orchid include Greenman's Hexalectris or Greenman's Cock's Comb.

While the signature plant species of the Edwards Plateau region are rare and unique on their own, together they help define the true nature of the Texas Hill Country. Monitoring and preserving them is not only good for the sake of maintaining biological diversity and understanding changing environmental conditions, but for the future beauty of our ecoregion as well.

Each tall, fleshy pink stalk of Spiked Crested Coralroot may bear up to 25 separate blooms.

The Giant Coralroot (Hexalectris grandiflora) *was recently found growing in the Balcones Canyonlands Preserve System.*

Wildflower Center

■ A shining jewel in our community is the Lady Bird Johnson Wildflower Center in South Austin (www.wildflower.org), whose mission is to "increase the sustainable use and conservation of native wildflowers, plants and landscapes." The center's gardens and sustainable architecture are not only a place of learning but a place of inspiration. Affiliated with several partners to promote the preservation and use of native plants, the center also offers spring and fall plant sales, Nature Nights for families, informative classes and workshops, and volunteer training and opportunities abound.

WHERE TO WATCH:

❖ Although many of these species are protected and are on private or access-restricted land, several of them can be seen at the Lady Bird Johnson Wildflower Center.

Meet the Salamanders

Amphibians such as salamanders, toads, and frogs are cold-blooded (ectothermic) animals that generally metamorphose from a water-breathing juvenile form to an air-breathing adult form. They are considered "ecological indicator" species, which means their health reflects the general health of their ecosystem. In recent decades, there has been a dramatic decline in amphibian populations worldwide, and many species have been declared threatened or extinct.

Rare and under threat of decreasing population, the U.S. Fish & Wildlife Service has stated that the Jollyville Plateau Salamander (*Eurycea tonkawae*) warrants protection under the Endangered Species Act, due to its habitat undergoing rapid degradation as a result of urban and suburban sprawl. Found only in the wet springs and caves of the Jollyville segment of the Edwards Plateau region of Travis and Williamson counties, the area this salamander inhabits is roughly bounded by the Colorado River, Mopac (Loop 1), Lake Travis, and U.S. 183. More specifically, its known range is limited to only six stream drainages, all of which are facing water quality issues.

Very little is known about this small, localized amphibian. Juvenile Jollyville Plateau Salamanders are less than 1½ inches long, and the adults grow to up to 2 inches long. They have large well-developed eyes, wide yellowish heads,

Jollyville Plateau Salamanders prefer cool, spring-fed, shallow waters.

The rare Jollyville Plateau Salamander is being considered for endangered species protection.

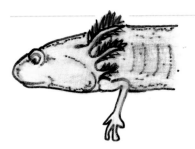

Feather-like gills of a stream salamander.

feathery external gills, blunt rounded snouts, dark greenish-brown bodies, and yellowish-orange tails. Most salamanders have feather-like external gills when they are young, but the Jollyville Plateau Salamander is neotenic, or keeps these external gills and remains aquatic for its entire adult life. Since they never take a terrestrial form, these salamanders prefer cool, shallow, clean water containing loose gravel. During drier periods, they remain in underground caves and water is provided for them by the infiltration of surface water through the soil into the aquifer which discharges from the springs as groundwater.

Urbanization has caused excess sediment to accumulate into the aquifer the salamanders inhabit and this sediment impairs their ability to avoid predators, locate food, and find mates. In addition, development upstream of salamander habitat provides sources of various other pollutants such as chemical fertilizers, pesticides, and petroleum products. During rainstorms, water runs off these urban areas and transports these pollutants into

The rare and endangered Barton Springs Salamander.

the salamander's aquatic habitat. This degradation of water quality has been linked to deformities of the Jollyville Plateau Salamander in some locations, as well as to declines in abundance of salamanders compared to areas that are undeveloped.

While the Balcones Canyonlands Preserve provides some water quality benefits for the Jollyville Plateau Salamander through the preservation of drainages in the open space, several of the areas within its range have been or are being affected by water quality degradation occurring upstream and outside of the preserved tracts. Work is being done to monitor and improve the areas within the preserve, but residents in neighborhoods surrounding the preserve can go a long way in helping to restore and maintain water quality by carefully disposing motor vehicle fluids, washing cars at a commercial car wash (where the water is captured and recycled), fertilizing wisely (organically), using compost, and planting native plants that have no need for chemical pesticides and herbicides.

The Barton Springs Salamander (*Eurycea sosorum*) is also quite rare, occurring only at the natural spring outflows of Barton Springs in downtown Zilker Park. Often found under rocks, in gravel, or hiding in aquatic plants in water up to 15 feet deep, these slender animals are about 2½ inches long with a narrow head, greatly diminished eyes, and external red gills with salt and pepper markings on their back. Often grayish-purple to yellow-brown in color, they eat tiny crustaceans and other small organisms, and rely on a clean, clear, continuous flow of spring water from the aquifer.

Listed as endangered in 1997, relatively little is known about the life history of these salamanders. Threats to its survival are directly related to water quality, which includes urban runoff, development along the Barton Creek watershed, and a decrease in groundwater supply due to increased usage. While swimming in Barton Springs Pool does not harm the Salamanders, certain maintenance procedures do, as well as removal of the aquatic plants on which they depend. The City of Austin monitors the Barton Springs salamander population on a monthly basis, and to date has acquired over 15,000 acres of land in the area that is preserved as open space. Much speculation occurs over the distribution of this salamander, since it is unknown how far it ranges into the aquifer. Accurate population estimates are also difficult to obtain, because the large rocks, crags, and surface area of the springs, in addition to the inaccessibility of the entire aquifer, make such an estimate virtually impossible.

Unlike our two local species of salamanders, the tendency of most terrestrial salamanders to dwell inside rotting logs is the source of numerous legends. When placed in a fire, the salamander would attempt to escape from the log, leading to the myth that salamanders were created from flames. This belief gave the salamander its name, as it literally means "fire lizard."

WHERE TO WATCH:

❖ As protected species, our native salamanders are rare and not to be disturbed, but you can learn about them and their habitat by visiting the exhibits like those at the "Splash! Into the Edwards Aquifer" at Barton Springs Pool and LCRA's Wilkerson Center at Redbud.

One of over 40 species of cicadas found in Texas, this common Annual Cicada (Tibicen resh), appears in the summer and the air sometimes vibrates with their loud songs.

CLIMATIC DATA FOR THE MONTH OF JULY IN AUSTIN.

	July 1	July 7	July 14	July 21	July 28
Record High	102°F	104°F	108°F	104°F	105°F
Average High	93°F	94°F	95°F	96°F	96°F
Average Low	73°F	73°F	73°F	74°F	74°F
Record Low	65°F	63°F	65°F	67°F	68°F
Sunrise	6:33 a.m.	6:35 a.m.	6:39 a.m.	6:43 a.m.	6:47 a.m.
Sunset	8:37 p.m.	8:36 p.m.	8:34 p.m.	8:32 p.m.	8:27 p.m.
Daylight	14 hr 4 min	14 hr 1 min	13 hr 56 min	13 hr 49 min	13 hr 40 min

Average Monthly Precipitation—2.16 inches

July

Water: The Essence of Life

Virtually every living thing on this planet requires water for survival, and the quality of that water is paramount. Austin is a key watershed area—rainwater flows over the land into our creeks, rivers, and lakes, and underground into the aquifer. This underground layer of porous rock, sand, or dirt contains large pockets of water, and water enters this aquifer through faults, sinkholes, caves, and other natural features on the surface to fill up or "recharge" the underground water supply. No matter how far away we are from a creek or a river, those of us who call Austin home live in one of 66 watersheds. As an example, much of the western part of our city is in the heart of the Bull Creek watershed, which is prime habitat for several endangered species. A famed Texas Ranger, Richard Lincoln Preece, killed the last remaining buffalo in Travis County along the banks of Bull Creek, giving it its name.

How we live in our watershed impacts our water quality, for humans and wildlife alike. Rain falling on our yards and streets carry pollutants such as chemical fertilizers and vehicle fluids into storm drains and creeks. As a result, water that is collected from the dammed-up Colorado River at Lake Austin must be treated before being drinkable, and water that continues down the river to the Gulf of Mexico carries those pollutants with it. Other sources of pollution include litter, hazardous chemicals dumped into storm drains, and even pet waste left on the ground.

One of the most effective ways to protect and improve water quality is to prevent pollution from your yard, home, and car. Use

An example of a storm drain marker tile.

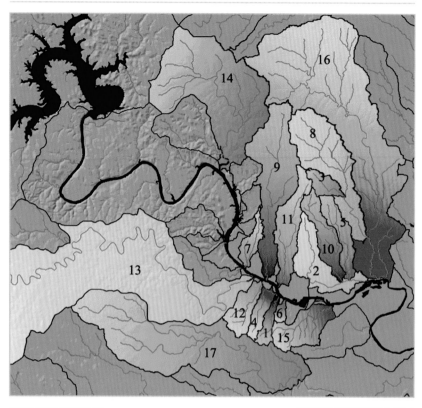

URBAN WATERSHEDS

1. Blunn (BLU)
2. Boggy (BOG)
3. Buttermilk (BMK)
4. East Bouldin (EBO)
5. Fort Branch (FOR)
6. Harper's Branch (HRP)

7. Johnson (JOH)
8. Little Walnut (LWAY)
9. Shoal (SHL)
10. Tannehill (TAN)
11. Waller (WRL)
12. West Bouldin (WBO)

NON URBAN WATERSHEDS

13. Barton (BAR)
14. Bull (BUL)
15. Country Club (CNT)
16. Walnut (WLN)
17. Williamson (WMS)

Map of Austin Area Watersheds—reprinted with permission from the City of Austin and the Watershed Protection Department.

only organic fertilizers and avoid chemical pesticides altogether. Plant native plants to conserve water and eliminate the need for pesticides, and use collected rainwater for irrigation. Pick up pet waste and dispose of it in a garbage can or toilet so the bacteria it carries is contained. Allow water to soak into the soil by using permeable materials for walkways and driveways. Dispose of all chemicals and paint products properly, and don't litter. Wash your car at a

The clear, cool waters of Bull Creek.

Barton Creek flowing along the Greenbelt.

car wash that filters, re-circulates, and reuses their water. Repair engine fluid leaks as soon as possible, and recycle used oil, filters, antifreeze, and all types of batteries.

If you'd like to get even more involved, the City of Austin has a plethora of projects, whether you want to volunteer individually or as a group. Examples include citizen monitoring of selected water quality testing sites, storm drain marking to help educate/remind citizens that storm drains flow directly into creeks, trash pickups, and most importantly, the Green Neighbor Program. This program provides you with all you need to know to help protect our water, and copies of the program booklet are available at all Austin libraries (or call 512–974–2550). Do

Clean Creek Challenge

■ As part of the Green Neighbor Program, the city encourages water quality awareness and active improvement through the Clean Creek Challenge (www.cityofaustin.org/watershed/cleancreek_main.htm). Adopting earth-wise habits is fun and easy through various programs, including organized Creek Cleanups, Adopt-a-Creek, and Storm Drain Marking Programs. Free copies of the Green Neighbor booklet are available at all Austin libraries.

your part and in return our creeks, rivers, and lakes will continue to be healthy sources of nourishment for all forms of life.

WHERE TO WATCH:

- ❖ Explore the Lower Colorado River Authority's (LCRA) Wilkerson Center at Redbud and Lake Austin Boulevard to learn about local water quality.
- ❖ Visit the trails along Bull Creek, Barton Creek, Walnut Creek, and Onion Creek, or take a guided hike hosted by the City of Austin's Wildland Conservation Division on one of the Water Quality Protection Lands (WQPL) properties.

Dazzling Dragonflies

With their large, multi-faceted eyes, two pairs of strong, transparent wings, and an elongated body, the dragonfly is an ancient insect that inspires myth

A Southern Maidenhair fern-lined tributary of Bull Creek.

and lore in many world cultures. For Native Americans, their form can represent swiftness and energy, pure water, and even symbolize renewal after a time of great hardship.

Usually found around lakes, ponds, streams, and wetlands, dragonflies typically eat mosquitoes, midges, and other small insects such as flies, bees, and even some butterflies and other dragonflies. They capture their prey by clasping them with their spike-studded legs, and their prey cannot use their usual form of escape by diving away, since dragonflies are quite agile and are quick to attack from any angle. Dragonflies are harmless to humans and are considered beneficial since they eat large numbers of flying insects, but their primary purpose is to reproduce.

The mating behavior of dragonflies is a multi-step process because the male has both a primary and secondary set of genitalia. He will first transfer sperm from the tip of his abdomen to the secondary structures on his second or third abdominal segment. Then, using the special structures at the tip of his abdomen, he will grab a receptive female by the back of her head. The pair is now considered to be in "tandem," and the male tows the female in flight. To complete the reproductive act, the female bends her abdomen beneath the male and touches the tip to the male's secondary structures. This position is called the copulation "wheel" and it is at this point when sperm is transferred to the female to fertilize her eggs.

The life cycle of a dragonfly consists of three stages: egg, larvae or nymph, and adult. After mating, the female will lay her eggs directly on aquatic plants or merely deposit them in water. Once hatched, these nymphs begin their life living underwater, eating other aquatic creatures. Nymphs of larger dragonflies will even eat the nymphs of smaller species. This nymphal stage can last as long as several years in some species, but most overwinter in ponds and

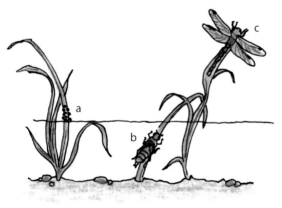

Dragonfly lifecycle: egg (a), larvae (b), and adult (c).

marshes and emerge the next spring as adults. Once fully grown, the nymph will crawl out of the water onto a rock or up the stem of a plant, break through its skin (called the "exuvia"), and enlarge its body and wings by pumping fluids into them.

Mature dragonflies are known for their aerial acrobatics, capable of hovering and rapid acceleration, and can both hunt and mate on the wing. They need to make the most of their time as aerial predators, since adults live only up to two months. Adult dragonflies are often confused with damselflies, but they are two distinct insect suborders. Primarily, wing shape is the most diagnostic feature, with all four wings of damselflies being equal, while the hindwings of dragonflies are broader than the forewings. When at rest, damselflies hold their wings together and sometimes slightly above their body, whereas dragonflies hold their wings fully open horizontally or slightly down and forward. Additionally, the eyes on a damselfly are separated, while the eyes of many (but not all) dragonflies touch. Both damselflies and dragonflies are members of the scientific order Odonata, so their life cycles are very similar.

The common names for dragonfly species that occur in Texas are as colorful as the insects themselves—Autumn Meadowhawk (*Sympetrum vicinum*), Roseate Skimmer (*Orthemis ferruginea*), Eastern Pondhawk (*Erythemis simplicicollis*), Black Saddlebags (*Tramea lacerata*), Stream Cruiser (*Didymops transversa*), Halloween Pennant (*Celithemis eponina*), and Blue Dasher (*Pachydiplax longipennis*) to name a few. To some extent, the presence of dragonflies may be taken as an indicator of ecosystem quality. Local populations and diversity may be strongly affected by changes in water flow, turbidity, and in aquatic or waterside vegetation. Not surprisingly, the greatest number of species is found at sites with natural water flows, high water quality, native plants, and a variety of microhabitats.

When you see dragonflies this summer, admire their maneuverability, enjoy their jewel-like colors, appreciate their mosquito-eating, and be thankful that we no longer have the "giant dragonflies" from the long-ago Jurassic and Cretaceous Periods, when their wingspans were up to six times larger than those we have today!

An adult male Roseate Skimmer has a bright pink abdomen.

The brilliant red color of a male Neon Skimmer (Libellula croceipennis) is easily recognized as it rests on its perch.

The Halloween Pennant is named for its orange and brown or black wings.

The Eastern Ringtail (Erpetogomphus designatus) has a yellowish-green thorax and a pale green face.

The American Rubyspot (Hetaerina americana) is a damselfly named for the red spots at the base of the male's wings.

Odonates Online

■ One of the most unique and informative websites for dragonfly identification is Digital Dragonflies (http://stephenville.tamu.edu/~fmitchel/dragonfly/). The award-winning technique used for photographing Odonata includes placing live-caught dragonflies overnight in the crisper drawer of a household refrigerator or in a plastic shoebox on one of the refrigerator shelves. Cold-sedated and with no loss of vibrant color often brought about by death, the dragonflies are then placed on a scanner in a cut out section of a mousepad, allowing the scanner lid to be closed without crushing the insect. Marvelously detailed images result, and best of all, the dragonflies quickly warm up and are released unharmed back into the wild.

Hosting the official website of the Dragonfly Society of the Americas, OdonataCentral is designed to "make available what we know about the distribution, biogeography, biodiversity, and identification of Odonata worldwide." Sponsored by the Texas Natural Science Center, OdonataCentral (www.odonatacentral.org) also hosts an excellent image library of dragonflies and damselflies, as well as checklists and maps of regional species.

Early morning dew sparkles on the wings of this female Sulphur-tipped Clubtail (Gomphus militaris).

It's easy to see how the Twelve-spotted Skimmer (Libellula pulchella) *received its common name.*

The powder blue abdomen and dark broad wingbands on both fore and hindwings are characteristic of the male Widow Skimmer (Libellula luctuosa).

This Four-spotted Pennant (Brachymesia gravida) *perches high on sticks and twigs.*

WHERE TO WATCH:

❖ Dragonflies prefer living near water sources surrounded by vegetation and can be observed at places like Hornsby Bend, Platt Lane, Riata Pond, and Bull Creek and Barton Creek greenbelts.

Edible Fruits and Berries

Among the key components of any healthy, natural habitat are the native plants that provide sustenance for wildlife. In the Austin area, there are several species that provide abundant fruits and berries during the warmer months, and many are edible for humans as well as wildlife.

Common in brushy areas, open woodlands, and stony hillsides, the Texas Persimmon (*Diospyros texana*) is a small tree (8–12 feet) that is moderately deer resistant. Flowering in March/April, this tree has little green leaves and attractive smooth pale reddish-gray bark that peels off to reveal a whiter trunk. The female trees bear 1 inch fruits that turn from green to black as they ripen in late July to September. Texas or Littleleaf Mulberry (*Morus microphylla*), also a large shrub or small tree, produces an edible fruit that is small, fleshy, and berry-like. Its color varies from red to black and it ripens in May, although in ideal conditions this tree can produce a large quantity of fruits over a longer period of time, providing much needed food for migrating and nesting birds.

Our native Escarpment Black Cherry (*Prunus serotina* var. *eximia*) is a fast-growing, straight-trunked tree with long clusters of white flowers in April/May,

Edible fruits and berries for humans include Escarpment Black Cherry (a), Texas Persimmon (b), Agarita (c), and Southern Dewberry (d).

112 *July*

followed by small purple-black cherries ripening in August through October. Although impractical for fresh eating, the cherries are used in juices and wines, and the bark was once used in making cough syrup. This deciduous tree is also unique in that it offers stunning yellow fall color. Another attractive tree is the Mexican Plum (*Prunus mexicana*), in which dense white flowers appear before the leaves in early spring, and offer a very sweet, heady scent. The plums, which ripen from July to September, are nearly as ornamental as the flowers, since their color varies widely from gold to crimson to purple-black.

Agarita (*Mahonia trifoliata*), a common native barberry, is a medium evergreen shrub whose gray-green holly-like leaflets are joined by yellow flowers in February/March and small red fruit in May through July. The leaflets have sharp points at the ends, so care must be taken to harvest the fruit, which makes an excellent jelly. Another sprawling shrub with thorny, woody stems is Southern Dewberry (*Rubus trivialis*) or Zarzamora. A bramble common to sunny meadows and open fields, its white flowers bloom in March/April, followed by berries that resemble blackberries but have a more sweet/tart flavor.

This Mexican Plum is beginning to ripen.

Mustang Grapes ripen to a deep violet-blue and can be eaten by humans and wildlife alike.

Edible and Useful Plants

■ *Edible and Useful Plants of Texas and the Southwest* by Delena Tull, is a practical guide to identification, recipes, natural dyes, harmful plants, and textile fibers of the plants in this area of the country. Of special note is the history behind the uses of many of our native Texas species, and is an excellent reference for those who wish to explore plant folklore and the deeper connection between humans and plants, as is *Remarkable Plants of Texas: Uncommon Accounts of Our Common Natives* by Matt Warnock Turner.

Usually found climbing along fencerows and high over other plants in woodland edges and stream sides is the Mustang Grape (*Vitis mustangensis*). Best used for wines and jellies, these vines can grow up to 40 feet long, and produce small clusters of acidic berries that ripen June through September, much to the delight of migrating birds.

Take some time this fall planting season to seek out and add some of these native fruit and berry plants to your landscape. Not only will you be providing food for several species of birds and mammals next year, but you'll have the chance to savor a natural and healthy treat for yourself, too.

WHERE TO WATCH:

❖ Often used for pies and cobblers and sold at fruit stands and farmers markets, Southern Dewberry is Texas' most popular wild berry and occurs naturally growing in thorny patches along roadsides, at the edges of thickets, and in fields.

❖ Agarita is very common in the Austin area, preferring the dry, rocky ground found in old pastures and shrubby areas. See if you can harvest the berries before the birds do!

❖ Look for the smooth gray trunks and branches of the Texas Persimmon and its sweet, dark fruit in thickets, open woodlands, and stony hillsides predominately in the western portion of the Austin area.

❖ NOTE: Please be cautious when determining whether or not a berry or fruit is toxic or edible as color alone is not a reliable factor. Be sure of your identification of the plant and refer to a reputable source such as Delena Tull's book or the Lady Bird Johnson Wildflower Center's online database as to its safety for human consumption.

Turtle Teachings

Hardly a day goes by in the summer months when you can't find a turtle basking in the sun. Like other reptiles, turtles are cold-blooded or ectotherms, who vary their internal temperature according to the ambient environment. Turtles have been around for over 250 million years, even longer than their snake and lizard relatives. We tend to use the word "turtle" for all freshwater and some land-dwelling species, while "tortoise" is used only to describe members of the true tortoise family.

The shell of a turtle has two parts: the upper is called the carapace, while the lower is called the plastron. Many turtles have a bony bridge that connects the top and bottom and lends strength and rigidity to the structure. Carapaces of turtles vary widely, and shape, colors, and patterns are among the field marks that distinguish one species from another. Scutes, from the Latin *scutum* or "shield," are the plates that cloak the outside of the turtle's shell. Most turtles have 54 scutes, with 38 covering the carapace, and 16 covering the plastron. Made from the protein keratin, scutes can be thought of as the epidermis covering the bony shell. It is even possible, by counting the stack of smaller, older scutes on top of the larger, newer ones, to estimate the age of a turtle. The accuracy of this method, however, is somewhat muddled by the variable growth rate of the scutes and the fact that, like fingernails or antlers, they eventually fall away from the shell.

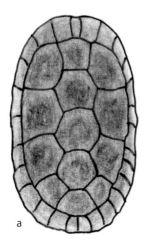 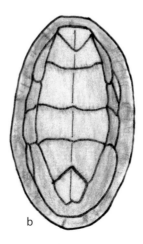

a   b

Structure of a carapace (a) and plastron (b), showing various types of scutes.

Regardless of the length of a turtle's neck, they all have eight vertebrae. In spite of their highly muscular necks, turtles are often called "hidden-necks," for their ability to retract their head and neck into the shell by bending it into a vertical S-curve and withdrawing from sight. Some species like box turtles go even further, and gain an added degree of protection from predators by having a hinge in their plastron, dividing it into two lobes, and giving them the ability to draw up those lobes and completely seal the turtle inside.

Turtles may spend most of their life in or around water, but they breathe air and often range widely when searching for a mate in the warmer months. With smell being the keenest sense possessed by a turtle, the males will chase any object of about the right size, and once close, will use smell to determine if the object is a female of the same species. Pregnant females dig a hole, often called a body pit, and deposit their eggs, covering them with dirt. In some species of turtles, temperature determines whether an egg develops into a male or a female, with higher temperatures producing females and lower temperatures producing males. Hatchlings squirm their way to the surface and head alone toward water, since there is no turtle species in which the female cares for the young.

The more common turtles in Central Texas include the Common Snapping Turtle (*Chelydra serpentina*), Three-toed Box Turtle (*Terrapene carolina trinuguis*), Red-eared Slider (*Trachemys scripta elegans*), Texas Map Turtle (*Graptemys versa*), and the Spiny Softshell (*Apalone spinifera emoryi*). All but the box turtle are generally found in wetlands, ponds, streams, and lakes where heavy vegetation is present, although box turtles are often activated by rain events. In late spring and early summer turtles wander, with males looking for mates and females searching for places to deposit and bury their eggs. If you find a turtle crossing the road (and if traffic allows for safety), move the turtle to the side where it is already headed. If it has been hit by a car, call Wildlife Rescue at 512–474-WILD (9453) or bring it to any emergency veterinary clinic.

Symbolically, the turtle has represented patience, strength, endurance, stability, and protection to many native peoples, who have observed the often slow but deliberate life of the turtle. This is a fascinating fact, since researchers have recently discovered that its major organs, such as the liver, lungs, and kidneys, do not gradually break down or become less efficient over time. Understandably, this has inspired geneticists to begin a detailed study of the turtle genome, hoping it can unlock the secrets of longevity.

Three-toed Box Turtles are hard to find in the wild, but can be seen at the Austin Science & Nature Center.

A Red-eared Slider basks in a pond at the Lady Bird Johnson Wildflower Center.

The Texas Spiny Softshell Turtle is named for a row of small projections or spines on the edge of the shell behind the head.

Box Turtle Survey Project

■ The Box Turtle Survey Project (www.tpwd.state.tx.us/learning/texas_nature_trackers/box_turtle_survey/) is part of Texas Nature Trackers, a collection of biological monitoring projects administered by Texas Parks & Wildlife and manned by trained volunteer citizen scientists. Box turtles (*Terrapene* sp.) are distinguished by other native Texas turtles by their hinged plastron and hooked or beaked upper jaw. Declining in numbers, you can help scientists and managers understand their population trends and management needs by reporting any sightings of the species.

The Ornate Box Turtle (Terrapene ornata ornata) *is related to the Three-toed Box Turtle but is distinguished by its darker carapace.*

WHERE TO WATCH:

❖ Aquatic turtles can be observed year-round at places like Lady Bird Lake and Hornsby Bend.

❖ Increasingly uncommon, the Three-toed Box Turtle prefers drier, upland wooded locations such as tracts of the Balcones Canyonlands Preserve System and further east in Bastrop State Park.

❖ Join the Box Turtle Survey project to find out more about box turtles and report your sightings of the species.

The Texas River Cooter (Pseudemys texana) *is a common but shy turtle, that will dive quickly into water when approached.*

A *Red-spotted Purple* (Limenitis arthemis) *butterfly rests on the leaf of a Mexican Plum tree.*

CLIMATIC DATA FOR THE MONTH OF AUGUST IN AUSTIN.

	August 1	*August 7*	*August 14*	*August 21*	*August 28*
Record High	106°F	108°F	105°F	107°F	104°F
Average High	96°F	97°F	96°F	96°F	94°F
Average Low	74°F	74°F	74°F	73°F	72°F
Record Low	63°F	67°F	65°F	62°F	64°F
Sunrise	6:49 a.m.	6:53 a.m.	6:57 a.m.	7:01 a.m.	7:05 a.m.
Sunset	8:25 p.m.	8:20 p.m.	8:13 p.m.	8:06 p.m.	7:58 p.m.
Daylight	13 hr 35 min	13 hr 27 min	13 hr 16 min	13 hr 5 min	12 hr 53 min

Average Monthly Precipitation—2.24 inches

August

Celestial Showers

Every August, one of the best-known meteor showers, the Perseid, makes its appearance. Comets shed the debris that becomes most meteor showers, and as comets orbit the sun, an icy, dusty stream of debris trails along the comet's orbit. If the Earth travels through this stream, we are treated to a meteor shower. Depending on where the Earth and the stream meet, meteors appear to fall from a particular place in the sky sometimes in the neighborhood of a constellation.

Meteor showers are usually named by the constellation from which the meteors appear to fall, a spot in the sky that astronomers call the radiant. The Perseid meteor shower is so named because the meteors appear to fall from a point in the constellation Perseus. The source of the shower is the comet Swift-Tuttle, the wide tail of which intersects the Earth's orbit even though the comet itself is nowhere near the Earth. As tiny bits of comet dust hit the Earth's atmosphere at 132,000 miles per hour, each makes a vivid streak of light when it disintegrates, and the shower is most intense when the Earth passes through in the dustiest part of the comet's tail.

Peak activity for the Perseid meteor shower is expected around the evening of August 12th, with a sharp increase in the hours after midnight. Assuming we have clear skies that night, escape the city's light pollution and find a dark, secluded spot where oncoming car headlights won't ruin your sensitive night vision. You'll know your eyes are

Perseus, the Greek hero, who killed Medusa and claimed Andromeda.

Timetable of major meteor showers

(Note that these are approximate times for the lower 48 states, actual times can vary.)

Name	Date of Peak	Moon Phase
Quadrantids	Morning of January 3	First Quarter
Lyrids	Night of April 21 Morning of April 22	Near New Moon
Eta Aquarids	May 5	Sets around 4 a.m.
Perseids	Morning/evening of August 12	Rises around midnight
Orionids	Morning of October 21	Near New Moon
Leonids	Night of November 17 Morning of November 18	New Moon
Geminids	Night of December 13/14	Near New Moon

properly adjusted and your site is dark enough if you can see each star of the Little Dipper constellation. Position yourself so that the horizon appears at the edge of your peripheral vision, with the northeast sky and the stars filling your field of view. Meteors will instantly grab your attention as they streak by.

A very good shower will produce around one meteor per minute per observer under a clear, dark sky. Any cloud cover, light pollution, or moonlight considerably reduces the count. The Perseids are among the strongest of the readily observed annual meteor showers, and at maximum activity will normally yield an average of 50 to 60 meteors per hour. In reality, what usually is seen is what some call the "clumping effect." Sometimes you'll see two or three meteors streak across the sky in quick succession, followed by a lull of several minutes before the sky suddenly puts on a display once again. While the Perseid meteor shower is an annual astronomical event, some years give us the opportunity for optimal viewing conditions if they happen to coincide with the new phase of the moon.

WHERE TO WATCH:

❖ Anywhere on the outskirts of the city, where light pollution no longer interferes with the dark skies needed for optimal meteor viewing.

❖ The Austin Astronomical Society (www.austinastro.org/) holds periodic star parties to view celestial events.

❖ Visit the University of Texas Painter Hall Telescope at West 24th Street and Inner Campus Drive, which is open for public viewings on Friday and Saturday evenings, http://outreach.as.utexas.edu/public/painter.html

Our most recognized constellation, the Big Dipper, is also called Ursa Major, meaning "big bear."

Amazing Arthropods

From the Greek roots of *arthron* (meaning "joint") and *podos* (meaning "foot"), arthropods are animals characterized by their jointed limbs and repeating body segments, each with a pair of appendages. They are so versatile that they have been called the "Swiss Army knives of species," and make up over 80 percent of all described living species known to date. In Central Texas, the most fascinating arthropods include the scorpion and the centipede.

Of the 90 species of scorpions identified in the United States, 18 occur in Texas but only one is found statewide. The number of species found increases as you move west and south in the state, with two species occurring in the Austin area compared to 14 in Big Bend National Park! Close relatives of ticks, mites, and spiders, scorpions are easily recognized by their shape, generally prefer dry habitats, hide during the day, and are most active at night.

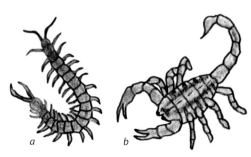

Segmented bodies of typical arthropods: centipede (a) and scorpion (b).

The most common scorpion in our area is the Striped Bark Scorpion (*Centruroides vittatus*), which has two broad, black bands running down the length of its back. Tan in overall color, this species can be easily identified by its slender pincer-bearing arms (pedipalps) and long, slender tail, which is longer on males than females. While these scorpions can mate in the fall, spring, or early summer, gestation requires about 8 months. Litter size varies from 13–47 young with an average litter of 31. Immature scorpions molt up to six times before they mature, with the first occurring anywhere from three to seven days after birth. Born alive in semi-transparent sacs, once they shed these thin layers they spend their first few weeks riding on their mother's back, and have a life expectancy of about 4 years.

Like all scorpions, the Striped Bark Scorpion has four pairs of legs with a comb-like sensory structure called the "pectines" between its last pair of legs. Although scorpions have two eyes on the top of the head and two to five pairs of eyes along the front corners of the head, they do not see well and rely on the pectines to identify different surface textures and to help detect prey. Their nocturnal habits assist them in managing temperature and water balance which are important functions for survival in dry habitats. The sting of this

The Striped Bark Scorpion is one of the most common scorpions in our area.

species is painful and can cause swelling, but none of the species in Texas are considered deadly. However, a person who has been stung should be watched for any adverse reaction.

Known as the largest centipede in North America, the Giant Redheaded or Texas Redheaded (*Scolopendra heros* var. *castaneiceps*) is a fast-moving, aggressive titan, among the largest of any many-legged centipedes in the world. While not frequently observed, those Texas Redheads that do make themselves known attract a lot of attention due to their large size and fierce appearance. They average about 6 to 8 inches in length and in rare cases may reach over 10 inches! Their coloration is striking, where the head and the first two body segments are dark red, the wide trunk is black tinged with green, and the first 20 pairs of legs are yellow. The posterior end of the centipede holds the twenty-first pair of legs, which are enlarged in size and mostly black with yellow tips. It is widely believed that this coloration advertises the species' poisonous qualities and confrontational nature and plays a key role in warding off potential predators.

Like the Striped Bark Scorpion, the Texas Redhead is a predator whose prey (primarily other insects) is captured and killed by its poison claws. Again, its bite, while painful, is not deadly to humans, but the same precautions should be taken.

Everything really is bigger in Texas, including this imposing Texas Redheaded Centipede!

Centipede or Millipede?

■ Centipedes differ from millipedes by the presence of only one pair of legs per body segment instead of two, and those legs are attached to the sides of each segment rather than near the midline. Additionally, centipedes generally have flattened versus rounded bodies, well-developed antennae on the head, and longer legs capable of rapid movement. Millipedes generally have shorter legs, and their movement is slow and wave-like.

While arthropods like scorpions and centipedes can be the source of nightmares and phobias for many people, their role in the ecosystem is one of extreme versatility. By examining the ways in which they are adapted to survive in a wide range of conditions, we learn that they are largely beneficial to us by keeping the balance of harmful insects in check, and when encountered, make for a Texas-sized story or two.

WHERE TO WATCH:

❖ Both scorpions and centipedes prefer hiding under rocks, fallen logs, and in leaf litter. Be careful where you place your hands when searching for these species!

Spiders on the Prowl

An often seen spider in our suburban yards and gardens is the Black and Yellow Garden Spider (*Argiope aurantia*). True to its common name, this spider has distinctive black and yellow (and sometimes orange) markings on its abdomen and a mostly white area behind its head. With a fairly rotund body of 1½ inches in length, the females of this species are twice as large as the males (common for most spiders), and can have colorful banding on the legs. These spiders are active during the summer months, and tend to be somewhat local, staying in one place throughout much of their lifetime. Like other members of this genus, they are considered harmless to humans.

These garden spiders have three claws on each foot, unlike most spiders that have only two claws, and the extra claw helps them spin complicated webs. Many times these webs are built in areas adjacent to open sunny areas, often 2 to 8 feet off the ground. Most distinctively, the circular part of their webs are

A Black and Yellow Garden Spider hangs from its newly created web, which shows the stabilimentum.

up to 2 feet in diameter, with a dense zigzag of silk, known as a "stabilimentum," in the center. While the purpose of this structure is disputed, it helps this spider earn its other common name, the writing spider. It is most often thought that the stabilimentum might warn birds of the presence of the web, and only those spiders that are active during the day construct these types of patterns in their webs.

Black and Yellow Garden Spiders breed once a year. The males roam in search of a female, building a small web near or actually in the female's web, then court the females by plucking strands on her web. When the male approaches the female, he often has a safety drop line ready, in case she attacks him. After mating, the male dies, and is sometimes then eaten by the female. The female will then lay her eggs, cover them with a sheet of silk, roll them into a sac, and hang them from the center of her web, where she spends most of her time. She guards the eggs against predation as long as she is able, but as the weather cools, she becomes frail, and dies around the time of the first hard frost. Come spring, the tiny young spiders exit the sac and disperse, often on a strand of silk carried by the wind.

Another common but startling-looking spider is the Spiny-backed Orbweaver, or Spiny Orbweaver (*Gasteracantha cancriformis*). Its shell is shaped like a crab shell, wide, flat and variably red, white, orange, or yellow with dark oval spots, rimmed by six red or orange spines. The males lack these distinctive spines, having only four or five stubby dark projections, and are two-thirds smaller than the females. Their Latin name comes from *cancer* meaning "crab" and *forma* meaning "shape, form, or appearance."

Also called a Jewel or Jewel Box Spider, the Spiny Orbweaver ranges across the southern half of the United States and is found year-round in woodland edges and shrubby areas of Texas. It usually adds decorations or little tufts of silk to its web, possibly to warn birds and other animals of the web's location. A short-lived spider, its lifespan lasts until reproduction in the spring following their birth. In fact, the males die only six days after mating with a female.

Often found feeding on flowers, the Green Lynx Spider (*Peucetia viridans*) is a bright green spider and the largest lynx spider in North America. The species name is derived from the Latin *viridis,* meaning "green," and is its signature characteristic. Its abdomen has a series of cream-colored chevrons

A typical spider form, showing the pedipalps (a), legs (b), cephalothorax (c), and abdomen (d).

A Spiny Orbweaver works on its web.

along its length, with white stripes accented by russet margins. Their long, thin legs are pale green to yellow, and are covered with long black spines and spots. Gravid or pregnant females are able to change color to fit their background, and depend on this ability in September and October, to help them defend their egg sac filled with bright orange eggs, from predation.

Active during late spring and summer in a wide variety of habitats, the Green Lynx Spider does not spin a web, but hunts for moths and other small insects among low shrubs and plants. This characteristic makes this spider of great interest for its use in agricultural pest management, but unfortunately it also preys on beneficial insects such as honey bees. Very seldom does this spider bite humans, and its bite is harmless.

Relatively common throughout Texas, Tarantulas (*Aphonopelma* sp.) are our heaviest and largest spiders. Typically, the head and legs are dark brown, and the abdomen is brownish-black. Coloration varies between individuals as well as among the 14 different species found in our state. Identification of species is difficult, however, and is often performed only on mature males under a laboratory microscope.

A Green Lynx Spider on a spiny Eryngo flower.

Venomous Spiders

▇ Two venomous spiders in the Austin area are the Southern Black Widow (*Latrodectus mactans*) and the Brown Recluse (*Loxosceles reclusa*). The female Southern Black Widow is a small, typically shiny black spider with a red hourglass-shaped marking on the underside of her abdomen. Even when disturbed in its web, which is an irregular mesh with a tent-like retreat and built low to the ground, this spider is quite timid and prefers to retreat rather than attack. Contrary to popular belief, she does not consume the male in most situations, except when confined together in a container from which the male cannot escape. They consume other insects, including the Red Imported Fire Ant. The Brown Recluse is shy, hiding in non-descript gray webs during the day, and hunting mostly at night. About an inch long with color varying from orange-yellow to dark brown, the Brown Recluse has six eyes arranged in three pairs in a semicircle in the front of the head. These eyes form the base of a violin-shaped marking on the back. The reaction to the venom from the bite of this spider can be immediate or delayed, but ultimately ends in killing the affected tissue.

Tarantulas are typically found in grasslands and semi-open areas, and use burrows, natural cavities under stones or fallen logs, spaces under loose tree bark, and even old rodent holes as shelters. They are also capable of digging their own burrows, and often line them with webbing, placing a few strands across the front to help detect passing prey. Laying several hundred eggs in a hammock-like web constructed inside the burrow, females will guard them until they hatch. Females have lived in captivity for over 25 years, while males rarely live over two or three months after reaching maturity.

Large and hairy, tarantulas prefer terrestrial burrows to building webs.

Other insects such as crickets, beetles, grasshoppers, cicadas, and caterpillars form the basic diet of the Tarantula. They inject their prey with a poison when they bite, liquifying the prey's insides, making it easier to ingest. While they can climb, they are usually restricted to the ground, with the males actively wandering in large numbers in late summer, apparently seeking out females. The hairiness and large size of Tarantulas often evokes concern, but the bites of Texas species are not serious to humans. Tarantulas maneuver quickly to face whatever disturbs them, often raising up on their hind legs and stretching out their front legs in a threatening posture. They have also been observed rapidly brushing the top of their abdomen with their hind legs to dislodge hairs that can be used to irritate the attacker's eyes or skin.

WHERE TO WATCH:

❖ Look for Black and Yellow Garden Spiders and Spiny Orbweavers on webs they string across pathways and between bushes in suburban yards.
❖ Green Lynx Spiders can be found on blooming plants, poised to strike at unsuspecting insects.
❖ Tarantulas are mostly ground-dwellers, and prefer rocky or grassy open areas where they can find cavities in which to den.

A typical karst feature in the Balcones Canyonlands Preserve System.

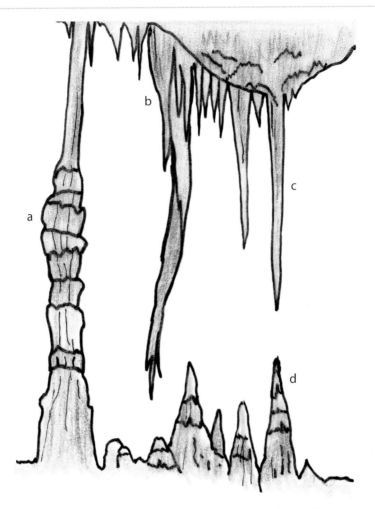

Features of a cave: column (a), drapery (b), stalactite (c), and stalagmite (d).

Caverns and Caves

Millions of years ago, the great seas that stood over Texas deposited the makings of thick layers of limestone. As the land rose and the seas fell, eons of rainfall leached out hollows, deep pits, and underground streambeds, and over time, these deeply hidden worlds built a silent beauty. Today, the state of Texas is riddled with over three thousand caves and sinkholes, most of them in the Edwards Plateau region.

The most important factor in cave formation is the presence of carbon dioxide in water, the main source of which is found in the soil. Rains form a weak carbonic acid that drives the progressive process of dissolution, a process that is more common in limestone than in any other type of rock. Fractures in the limestone allow this weak acidic water to fill voids in the rock, and as the water flow eventually decreases and the water table recedes, caves may become dry or partially dry.

Some of the carbon dioxide that was in the water is released into the cave atmosphere, causing the water to become less acidic, and the calcium carbonate dissolved in it begins to form tiny crystals or precipitate. Individual crystals build upon one another, and a steady drip from a cave ceiling can create a wide variety of cave formations. There are downward-building stalactites, upward-growing stalagmites, and if the two grow together they can form a column. Ribbons of stone can develop into shapes resembling draperies, curtains, soda straws, coral, pearls, and even strips of bacon.

The unusual and ever-changing environment of a cave with its constant darkness, temperature, and relative humidity creates unique and interesting inhabitants. Scientists believe that many are relict species, isolated populations that were left to follow their own evolutionary path. Those species truly adapted to caves have reduced eyes and pigment, slender bodies, and extra long legs, which allows the animal to spread itself over a larger surface area in such a food-poor environment. These extreme adaptations can be seen in many of Central Texas' threatened and endangered species such as cave salamanders, beetles, spiders, pseudoscorpions, and other cave invertebrates. Several species of bats inhabit Texas caves—with almost 100 million individuals in about a dozen caves—and they routinely leave the caves in search of food thereby showing the least adaptation and restriction to these environments.

Many Central Texas caves are "wild" and explored mainly by expert cavers, geologists and biologists, but seven caves are considered "show" caves, or caves that have been developed enough to be enjoyed by the general public. Natural Bridge Caverns, located north of San Antonio, is the largest commercial cave in Texas, and full of draperies, curtains, stalagmites, and stalactites. Cascade Caverns in Boerne, otherwise known as the "Peep in the Deep," has a 90-foot waterfall when conditions are wet. Wonder World Cave in San Marcos is the oldest commercial cave in Texas, where you can find ceilings full of fossils and directly view the waters of the Edwards aquifer as well as the underside of the Balcones fault line. Longhorn Caverns in Burnet was used for shelter by the Comanche Indians and for worship by a local church, and has large calcite crystals filling its walls. Inner Space Caverns in Georgetown features soda straw ceilings and an underground theater for educational programs. The Caverns of Sonora, a short drive from Sonora, was designated a National Natural Landmark in 1966, and is one of the most active caves in the world, with over 95 percent of its formations still growing. The Cave Without a Name, just northeast of Boerne, holds the state's best examples of cave bacon, one of which is almost 22 feet long!

As unique features of the land, caves are protected by Texas law, and benefit from the stewardship of cavers, cave owners, and the general public. Marvel at the formations (but don't touch), seek to understand their origins, and remember, summer is the perfect time to get out of the Texas heat by heading down into a cave.

WHERE TO WATCH:

❖ Visit the show caves in the surrounding area or join the Austin Speleological Survey for information on local caving.

❖ Explore Westcave Preserve, a natural treasure of the Texas Hill Country, 40 miles southwest of Austin (www.westcave.org).

❖ With their constant year-round temperature, caves can be explored at any time of year, but are celebrated every year in March with the Austin Cave Festival hosted by the Barton Springs/Edwards Aquifer Conservation District (www.bseacd.org/events/austin_cave_festival).

A Polyphemus Moth is easily attracted to our back porch lights.

CLIMATIC DATA FOR THE MONTH OF SEPTEMBER IN AUSTIN.

	September 1	September 7	September 14	September 21	September 28
Record High	107°F	101°F	102°F	100°F	106°F
Average High	93°F	92°F	91°F	89°F	87°F
Average Low	72°F	71°F	69°F	68°F	66°F
Record Low	59°F	54°F	54°F	50°F	49°F
Sunrise	7:08 a.m.	7:11 a.m.	7:15 a.m.	7:19 a.m.	7:23 a.m.
Sunset	7:54 p.m.	7:46 p.m.	7:38 p.m.	7:29 p.m.	7:20 p.m.
Daylight	12 hr 46 min	12 hr 35 min	12 hr 23 min	12 hr 10 min	11 hr 57 min

Average Monthly Precipitation—3.42 inches

September

Is the Only Good Snake a Dead Snake?

bsolutely not! Although snakes are animals like any other animal, most people do not see snakes in this way. Many people have an unfounded fear of snakes, and think they should be killed, due to myths and other untruths that are prevalent in our society. Snakes do not come onto our property to hurt us, our family, or our pets. They are generally in search of a place to carry out their daily lives—like all animals, they need places to hide, build a nest, catch food, or find a mate.

If you see a snake on your property, leave it alone. Chances are, it is much more afraid of you than you are of it, and it will leave on its own. Over time, if

A Redstripe Ribbon Snake (Thamnophis proximus rubrilineatus) *glides along the lilypads on the surface of a pond.*

you continue to see snakes on your property, call a humane removal service like Austin Reptile Service (512–837–6253) that will rescue and relocate the snake, remove its prey (which is most likely why the snake is there in the first place), and help you snake-proof your home.

Many people don't realize that snakes serve an important role in the ecosystem. They benefit humans by eating rodents like mice and rats, and insects, which can carry harmful diseases that can cause illness or in some rare cases even death. And not all snakes are poisonous. According to Texas Parks & Wildlife, humans are four times more likely to get killed by a lightning strike than by a poisonous snakebite. Of those found in Texas, only four types of snakes are poisonous (rattlesnake, copperhead, cot-

a

b

The author with a large (7 feet long) Western Coachwhip (Masticophis flagellum testaceus) *skin found near RM 2222.*

Pattern differences help distinguish between the venomous Coral Snake (a) and various species of harmless milk snakes (b).

tonmouth, and coral snake) and over 100 species/subspecies are non-venomous and harmless.

Some non-venomous species common to Central Texas and mistakenly identified as rattlesnakes include the Texas Rat Snake (*Elaphe obsoleta linheimeri*) and the Bullsnake (*Pituophis catenifer sayi*). The Texas Rat Snake is the most common large snake in the Austin area. While juveniles are colored with brown blotches on a gray background, the dark gray to black blotches of the adults will be on a red, orange, or even yellow background, giving it a wide range of color combinations. Found in the eastern two-thirds of the state, this snake grows to 4 to 6 feet on average, can be aggressive when cornered, and even vibrates its tail to mimic a rattlesnake. Due to specialized, sharp-edged scales on their belly, they are excellent climbers and these constrictor snakes can prey on birds and bird eggs, but prefer to eat rodents. The Bullsnake is also a very common large snake (4 to 6 feet when mature), and is identified by almost square brown blotches on a light brown or yellow background. Because they are heavy-bodied snakes that move slowly, they are frequently killed when crossing roads. They typically hunt during the day, except when warm summer temperatures force them to delay their activity to the twilight and dawn hours. They hiss very loudly and even snort when threatened, hence earning their common name.

Other smaller but also common non-venomous snakes include the Eastern Black-necked Garter Snake (*Thamnophis cyrtopsis ocellatus*) and the Rough Green Snake (*Opheodrys aestivus*). Usually found around gardens and near springs and permanent water sources, the Eastern Black-necked Garter Snake is slender, 2 to 3 feet long, and identified by a black head/neck with a bright orange center line down its mostly black back and pale yellow side stripes. Its diet consists of frogs, toads, fish, tadpoles and other aquatic or semi-aquatic prey. Uniformly leaf-green in color with an ivory belly, the Rough Green Snake averages 2 to 2½ feet long. Feeding on spiders, caterpillars, grasshoppers, and crickets, these graceful creatures are usually found near water or damp woodlands and grassy areas.

If you are interested in identifying snakes in Texas, be careful to learn from an expert or club such as the Austin Herpetological Society (www.austinherpsociety.org), and remember to give snakes the respect they deserve as they are a vital part of a healthy ecosystem.

The Texas Rat Snake, like this one at the Austin Nature & Science Center, is an excellent climber.

Non-venomous Bullsnakes are often mistaken for rattlesnakes.

An Eastern Black-necked Garter Snake emerges from his rocky den.

WHERE TO WATCH:

❖ Take care as you seek out the very common Bullsnake and similar looking rattlesnake, generally reclusive but most often seen sunning themselves in the early morning hours in the drier, upland habitats that are rocky and sparsely vegetated. Generally, you will see one when you least expect it!

❖ Other non-venomous snakes can often been seen as they search for prey in damp areas or near small ponds such as human-made retention ponds near several of our highways and the numerous water features at the Lady Bird Johnson Wildflower Center.

Hoppin' Orthoptera

Take a walk through a meadow on a warm summer day, and you'll no doubt encounter members of the insect order Orthoptera: grasshoppers, crickets, and katydids. While their Greek name translates to *straight wings,* these insects are better known for their jumping ability and powerful hind legs that can propel them up to 20 times their body length.

Abundant, large, colorful, and often noisy, orthopterans are unlike other insects in that they undergo an incomplete or gradual metamorphosis. Their simple lifecycle consists of an egg, nymph, and adult, where the nymphs look similar to adults, but lack completely developed wings. Eggs typically hatch in the spring, nymphs develop through the summer, and adults mate and reproduce in late summer and fall, with winter passing in the egg stage. They have three basic body parts: the head, which contains sensory parts such as antennae, eyes, and mouthparts; the thorax, which contains the legs and wings required for movement; and the abdomen, which bears the digestive and reproductive organs.

The use of sound is crucial in the courtship of these insects, with each

Grasshoppers have short antennae shaped either like a sword (a) or a club (b). Crickets and katydids have long, thread-like antennae (c).

species having its own distinctive song. Males attract mates through stridulation, or producing sounds by rubbing the upper and lower wings or the hind leg and wing together creating a vibration that is species-specific. The auditory organs for orthopterans are not located on their heads, however, but on the abdomen for grasshoppers and the front legs of crickets and katydids.

A common group of grasshoppers in the Austin area are the Band-winged Grasshoppers (*Arphia* sp.). Heavy-bodied with large hind legs and rounded heads with vertical faces, these grasshoppers are typically 1 to 1½ inches long, grayish-brown to black and mottled with numerous spots. When they fly, their open hind wings show a bright orange-red, the only give away to the natural camouflage of their grassy habitat. The Differential Grasshopper (*Melanoplus differentialis*) is brown to olive-green and yellow and up to 1¾ inches long, with black herringbone markings on its legs. It feeds on both grasses and broadleaf plants, although it prefers the latter. A close cousin, the Eastern Lubber Grasshopper (*Romalea microptera*) is large and has a variable color pattern of yellow, red, and black, showing rose-colored forewings when in flight. Most often found in low moist areas with dense undergrowth, when alarmed this grasshopper will hiss, spread its wings, and secrete a foul-smelling froth from its spiracles, the breathing structures on the sides of its abdomen.

More often heard than seen, Tree Crickets (*Oecanthus* sp.) are whitish to light green, with long antennae and slender bodies. In late summer from dusk into the evening hours, the males begin to chirp, with the rate of the chirp correlating to the outside temperature. If you count how many chirps you hear in

Differential Grasshoppers love to eat Giant Ragweed (Ambrosia trifida *var.* texana) *and Common Sunflower* (Helianthus annuus)*, and can travel up to a few miles in search of food.*

15 seconds and add that to 40, you'll come surprisingly close to the actual air temperature in degrees Fahrenheit. Field Crickets (*Gryllus* sp.) are dark brown to black, about 1 inch long, live in cool, dark areas, and normally emit high-pitched, continuous calls. Those that live in caves are dark brown, have well-developed hind legs, and exhibit a hunchbacked appearance. The Southern Mole Cricket (*Scapteriscus borellii*) is a subterranean insect, with shovel-like front legs

modified for digging. Dull brown and cylindrical, they are poor jumpers but fly at night and are quick runners.

The antennae of katydids are hair-like and at least as long as the body, superbly represented by the True Katydid (*Pterophylla camellifolia*). The common name for these green insects is derived from their calls, typically rendered as a harsh *ka-ty-did, she-did, she-didn't,* and heard from early summer through early fall. Abundant and living in open, grassy meadows, the calls of the male Texas Bush Katydid (*Scudderia texensis*) include a long but irregularly spaced, fast-paced song in late afternoon, followed by a soft ticking sound at the onset of evening twilight, and ending with a slow-pulsed song that becomes prominent as darkness sets in.

Often, what you can't identify by sight during the day becomes clear when it sings, calls, buzzes, or chirps at night. Close your eyes, immerse yourself in the nighttime soundscape, and hear your way to a whole new world of discovery.

Male Field Crickets begin chirping in mid- to late summer, looking for a mate.

Prophets and Phantoms

▧ Several Praying Mantis species (for example, *Stagmomantis* sp. and *Tenodera* sp.) occur in Texas. These green insects have front legs designed for grasping prey, and they hold them in such a way that mimics praying. As such, they are often called "prophets," and are considered a beneficial insect in that they are a natural predator that feeds on other insects, including each other. Walkingsticks (*Anisomorpha* sp.) are slow-moving, wingless, stick-like insects with long thread-like antennae. Members of the order Phasmatodea (meaning "phantom"), they are an excellent example of the evolution of mimicry, with most species varying from brown to green and about 4 inches long. The one exception is the Giant Walkingstick (*Megaphasma dentricus*), the longest insect in the United States with females that can grow up to 7 inches.

WHERE TO WATCH:

❖ Grassy fields, meadows, and roadsides, such as those found in the City of Austin's WQPL tracts and in open areas of our city parks and preserves.

The female Texas Bush Katydid listens for the long song of its mate, which he sings at dusk.

September 145

Hummingbird Highways

One of the most plentiful jewels in Texas, the Black-chinned Hummingbird (*Archilochus alexandri*) may be small, but its fall migration is a feat of gigantic proportions! Measuring a mere 3½ inches long with a 3¾ inch wing span, this hummingbird weighs only 3 to 3½ grams, which is about equivalent to the weight of a dime plus a dollar bill. The male is dull metallic green above, gray below, black on the chin and upper throat, with an iridescent violet lower throat known as a gorget (pronounced gore-JET). The female lacks the characteristic coloring on the chin, upper throat, and lower throat.

Like all hummingbirds, nectar serves as its main food source, fueling the tiny bird's extreme metabolism. These hummingbirds feed on several species of plants, most notably members of the native penstemon, agave, salvia, sage, and honeysuckle families. While artificial feeders supplement their diet, they also prey on small insects and spiders, particularly during nesting season, which gives them the dietary fat and protein necessary to breed.

The Black-chinned Hummingbird's unique skeletal structure allows them to fly forward, backward, sideways, and even on their backs. This requires a wingbeat frequency of about 50 beats per second, and massive muscles that make up a third of their tiny body weight. The males perform an elaborate flight display during courtship, but no pair bond is formed between the males and females. Females build the diminutive nest out of spider webs, mosses, and various plant fibers, incubate the eggs, and raise the young, while the males are feeding and off chasing other females. This is unusual among birds as a group, because, unlike other vertebrates (animals with a backbone or spinal column), birds are frequently monogamous.

While most biologists believe that the shortening length of daylight hours triggers fall migration, the Black-chinned Hummingbird begins its long journey south from Texas in September, to spend the winter in Western Mexico. The number of birds migrating south may be twice that of the northward trip in the spring, since it includes all immature birds that hatched during the summer, as well as surviving adults.

Most often seen during migration accompanying the Black-chinned Hummingbird, the Ruby-throated Hummingbird (*Archilochus colubris*) is a more eastern species. Nearly identical in size and shape to Black-chinned Hummingbirds, the males are identified by their brilliant ruby-red throats.

A male Black-chinned Hummingbird showing the purple band at the bottom of his gorget.

A male Ruby-throated Hummingbird hovers near a feeder.

a   b

While Black-chinned and Ruby-throated Hummingbird males
can be identified by the color of their gorgets, females require
a closer look at their tail feathers. Black-chinned (a) has a
rounded tail, and Ruby-throated (b) has a double-rounded tail.

They are found in open, mixed woodlands and meadows and winter mostly in Costa Rica and El Salvador, with some birds wintering in coastal Texas.

Amazingly, for a newly hatched hummingbird, there is no memory of past migrations, only an unexplained urge to put on a lot of weight, fly in a particular direction for a certain amount of time and hundreds of miles, and look for a good place to over-winter. Once it learns such a route, a bird may retrace it every year as long as it lives. There is evidence that fall and spring migration routes differ, with the hummingbirds following the Texas coast back into Mexico in the fall and crossing non-stop over the Gulf of Mexico on their way north in the spring. Perhaps the hurricane season is a factor, and these birds have developed an innate sense to avoid the Gulf during the fall, its most precarious weather season.

The timing of the fall hummingbird migration occurs when their natural food is most abundant. However, you can enjoy this amazing spectacle up-close by keeping your feeders full of clear, fresh sugar water through at least the end of October, and enjoying the company of these enchanting little gems as they make a rest stop in your yard on their way to their winter home.

WHERE TO WATCH:

❖ Generally speaking, you will find Black-chinned Hummingbirds at tubular red flowers west of the Balcones escarpment, and Ruby-throated Hummingbirds east of the Balcones escarpment.

Proper Feeding of Hummingbirds

■ The nectar from over 100 plant species used by hummingbirds is primarily made up of a combination of sucrose (table sugar), fructose, and glucose. Small amounts of protein are also present, but most hummingbirds can get that protein by eating insects for a short time each day. While natural nectar is the preferred energy source for hummingbirds, when presented with just one sugar they prefer sucrose. Proper feeding of hummingbirds with a feeder requires a water-to-sugar ratio of 4:1 to promote optimum feeding activity and provide sufficient energy. Although the color red attracts hummingbirds, it should be present as part of the feeder and not an additive to the sugar solution. Feeders should be cleaned frequently to prevent mold and fungus growth and the sugar solution should be replaced every few days especially in warmer weather.

❖ Reference the book *Hummingbirds of Texas* by Cliff Shackelford, Madge Lindsay, and Mark Klym, published by Texas A&M University Press.
❖ Join the Texas Hummingbird Roundup (www.tpwd.state.tx.us/learning/texas_nature_trackers/hummingbird_roundup/) to help wildlife biologists learn more about Texas hummingbirds and their relationship to their habitat.
❖ Invite hummingbirds to your own garden by providing nectar with native, blooming plants and supplemental feeders.

Mysterious Moths

While much more numerous but not as widely studied as their close cousins the butterflies, moths are a large and fascinating group of insects. Making up about 80 percent of the insect order known as Lepidoptera, most moths are active mainly at night, strangely attracted to light, and while some never eat, many species can live much longer than most butterflies and can even hibernate over the winter.

Like butterflies, the life cycle of a moth is comprised of an egg, caterpillar (larvae), pupa, and adult. The length of this cycle and each of its phases varies among species, with some species producing as many as ten broods a year. Many moths have hairy bodies to help maintain the internal body temperature necessary for flight, and heat up their flight muscles by vibrating their wings, since they don't have the radiant energy of the sun to assist them.

Sphinx Moths or Hawk Moths, whose wings beat 70 times per second, have a top speed of 50 kilometers per hour, and even more amazingly, many pupate underground! Moths range in size from the micros that have wingspans of 3 to 4 millimeters to the female Cecropia Moth, with a record wingspan of over 6 inches, the largest insect in North America.

Moths are positively phototactic, or automatically move toward a source of light. While the exact reason for this is unknown, interesting theories abound. Some moths are known to migrate short distances, and may use the night sky to navigate. They may use the moon as a primary reference point and have the ability to calibrate their flight paths as the moon moves across the night sky. This may help orient them, and can also explain the disorientation they seem to experience when they unexpectedly "catch" or fly above a light source that they think is the moon. It is also possible that moths look at light as an escape route mechanism, where flying up toward the light signifies safety, and flying down toward the darkness signifies danger.

Once they find an appealing source of light (preferring white versus yellow wavelengths), moths seem entranced by it. Like humans, moth's eyes contain light sensors, but unlike humans their dark-adapting mechanism responds much more slowly than their light-adapting mechanism. This could mean that they may not want to leave the light since the dark renders them blind for so long, and might explain why they can be attracted to the light over and over again. Lastly, since moths are generally nocturnal creatures, they may respond to the light like they would the rising sun, and settle in for a good day's sleep.

With so many thousands of moth species, even the largest can be difficult to identify. Clues can be gleaned from their profile or posture, vein patterns in their wings, and even the time of night that they are most active. Moths have antennae that are either feather-like or hair-like, and the male's feather-like antennae are larger than the female's. Using these antennae, the male can detect a female from as much as 5 miles away since unmated females release pheromones, a chemical trigger used to attract members of the same species. Some of our most beautiful nighttime jewels include the Cecropia, Imperial, Luna, and Polyphemus moths. These large moths, all members of the giant silkworm or Saturniidae family, hold our greatest fascination. Born without any mouthparts, the adults of this family never eat or drink and their sole purpose is to reproduce.

As one of the largest moths in North America, the Cecropia Moth's (*Hyalophora cecropia*) stout larvae grow to about 4 inches long and can actually

be heard when eating. Un-
like other moths in the same
family, there is only one larvae
or caterpillar brood per year,
pupating into a double-layered
cocoon, which allows them to
overwinter in that stage and
emerge as adults the following
spring. Identified by its large
red body, white collar, brown-

Some field marks of a generalized moth:
forewing (a), hind wing (b), antenna (c),
reniform spot (d), orbicular spot (e).

ish wings each with a red crescent and a stripe, and two dark eyespots on the
forewings, this large moth is often found roosting during the day.

In a different subfamily is the Imperial Moth (*Eacles imperialis*), who like
other members of this subfamily pupate underground. Adults emerge before
sunrise, and mate after midnight the following day. In the south they emerge
at various times between April and October. While there is a high degree of
variation of the coloration of the adults, all are combinations of yellow and
purple. Males have considerably more purple than the females, especially on
the forewing, but both are found mostly on oaks in our area.

Cecropia Moths are some of the largest flying insects.

Often sought after, the Luna Moth (*Actias luna*), is a large, otherworldly, pale-green, gentle giant. Dark pink or reddish-brown at the outer margins, with a translucent eyespot on the forewings and a sweeping tail on the hindwings, this moth has an average wingspan of 3 to 4 inches and is 5 to 6 inches long. Not to be mistaken for any other North American moth, this relatively common beauty is seldom seen but never forgotten. Having up to three broods from March to September here in the south, its larval host plants include willow, walnut, cherry, and pecan trees. The most ethereal of all the moths, mating occurs over the course of four hours. Adults emerge in the morning, with the sole purpose of reproducing, and only live about one week.

With a wingspan of about 6 inches, the Polyphemus Moth (*Antheraea polyphemus*) is light tan to sandy-colored and most easily recognized for the large purple eyespots on its hindwings. Taken individually, each eyespot was a reminder of the Greek myth of the cyclops Polyphemus, who only had one eye. Caterpillars of this species have been observed to eat 86,000 times their weight

The Luna Moth is one of the most ethereal of all wild creatures.

in two months after emerging, mainly in the form of oak, willow, cherry, and walnut leaves. To protect itself from predators, the adult moth will flash its hindwings, with the eyespots acting as a distraction pattern to confuse those who wish to eat it.

While not a member of the giant silkworm moth family, the Black Witch Moth (*Ascalapha odorata*) has been known as *mariposa de la muerte* or "butterfly of death" since the time of the Aztecs. With a wingspan of up to 6 inches, it is one of the largest moths that occur north of Mexico. Females are slightly larger and lighter in color than males, and have a pale almost lavender-pink median band through both fore- and hind wings. Common to abundant in the New World topics as far south as Brazil, the Black Witch flies year-round in South Florida and the Rio Grande Valley of Texas. The summer monsoons in Mexico prompt this fabulous creature to migrate north through Texas, where it is often found in our area in garages, under eaves, or under bridges.

Primarily nocturnal, the Black Witch is attracted to light and fermenting

A Polyphemus Moth, showing its signature eyespots.

This Black Witch Moth rested under the eaves of our front porch for several hours.

Attracting Moths

■ One easy way to attract moths is to set up a light at night. Often called "black-lighting," different types of lights can be used, although black and mercury vapor lights are the most effective. Hang the bulb in front of a vertical white sheet or cloth in your backyard or near a woodland edge, and turn it on at dusk. Check it after 3 or 4 hours and you should find a myriad of moths perched on the sheet. Don't forget to turn the light off and shake the sheet clean before morning, however, or you will provide the early birds with a very easy meal!

Baiting or "sugaring" is another tried and true method to attract and observe moths. Often attracting species that do not respond well to blacklighting, creating a sugar trail often works well in our dry oak-juniper woodlands. Bait concoctions vary widely, but most are based on brown sugar, stale beer, and overripe fruit (such as bananas or peaches). Blend them together, allow the mixture to ferment a few days, and you've got yourself some moth bait. Use a paint brush to apply the mixture at eye-level in foot-square patches, to a series of trees along a trail. Mark the trees with fluorescent tape so that when night falls, you can find them with your flashlight. Moths, the mysterious majority, will nectar on these trees at night, and you should be able to observe them as long as you are quiet and don't shine your flashlight directly on them.

fruit. Its larvae feed at night on a variety of cassias, acacias, and other woody legumes, and rest during the day on bark and branches. Up to 3 inches long, the caterpillar is dark gray tinged with brown, with a pale stripe down the back and dark stripes down the sides, and relies on this natural camouflage to make it difficult to spot. Pupation occurs on the ground in scattered leaf litter within a fragile cocoon. At first glance, this very large moth is often mistaken for a small bat hovering around a porch light, but it will eventually land and linger for several hours. If this happens to you, you can only hope that the legend of the Black Witch in South Texas is true: "If a Black Witch lands above your door and stays there for a while, you could win the lottery!"

WHERE TO WATCH:

❖ Consider leaving your porch lights on deep into the night, or better yet, set up a blacklighting station or prepare a sugar trail to attract and observe moths in your own yard during the overnight hours.

❖ During the summer months, the Austin Butterfly Forum, (www.austinbutterflies.org/home), often sets up a blacklighting station to observe moths during their evening monthly meetings. This local club conducts butterfly counts, promotes butterfly gardening, offers field trips, performs conservation activities, and meets monthly for an educational presentation. Not limited to butterflies, members are also very interested in dragonflies, moths, and other fascinating members of the insect world.

A Monarch butterfly feeds on a Woolly Butterflybush (Buddleja marrubiifolia).

CLIMATIC DATA FOR THE MONTH OF OCTOBER IN AUSTIN.

	October 1	*October 7*	*October 14*	*October 21*	*October 28*
Record High	98°F	97°F	95°F	92°F	89°F
Average High	86°F	84°F	82°F	80°F	77°F
Average Low	65°F	63°F	61°F	58°F	56°F
Record Low	42°F	47°F	42°F	39°F	32°F
Sunrise	7:24 a.m.	7:28 a.m.	7:32 a.m.	7:37 a.m.	7:42 a.m.
Sunset	7:16 p.m.	7:09 p.m.	7:01 p.m.	6:54 p.m.	6:47 p.m.
Daylight	11 hr 52 min	11 hr 41 min	11 hr 29 min	11 hr 16 min	11 hr 5 min

Average Monthly Precipitation—3.23 inches

October

Magical Monarch Migration

Most of us are aware of the typical life cycle of a butterfly—first an egg is laid on a food plant, a caterpillar or larva hatches from the egg, once the caterpillar eats enough it turns into a chrysalis, and shortly after a beautiful adult butterfly emerges. However, unlike other butterflies, migration plays a key role in the Monarch's lifecycle, and it is a fantastic migration at that!

Unlike most other insects in temperate climates, Monarch butterflies (*Danaus plexippus*) cannot survive a long, cold winter. Instead, they spend the winter in one of two main roosting spots—those west of the Rockies travel to

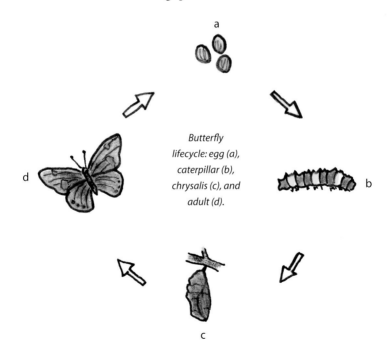

Butterfly lifecycle: egg (a), caterpillar (b), chrysalis (c), and adult (d).

Monarch butterflies, and their close cousins the Queens, love to nectar on Blue Mistflowers.

small groves of trees along the California coast, and those east of the Rockies fly further south to the forests high in the Sierra Madre Mountains of Central Mexico.

Austin is on the very eastern edge of this central flyway to Mexico, and in October and November large numbers of Monarchs work their way through Central Texas. Most of these butterflies were actually born on milkweed plants in Canada earlier in the summer. Even though they look like summer adults, they won't mate or lay eggs until the following spring. Instead, their small bodies prepare for a strenuous flight. As they migrate south, the Monarchs stop to nectar, and actually gain weight in the form of fat to fuel their flight and last them throughout their winter roost. These butterflies wake up about mid-morning, gather nectar from flowers in full bloom, then fly until sunset covering distances up to 400 miles in a single day. Although this generation of butterflies has never ventured into Mexico in the past, somehow they still find their way.

Once they reach their wintering grounds in Mexico, the Monarchs roost in huge clusters that virtually drip off the evergreen trees, and feed on the nectar

Antelope Horns (Asclepias asperula), or Spider Milkweed, is a native milkweed plant that grows in clusters among grasses in our area.

Tropical Milkweed, (Asclepias curassavica) a favorite of the Monarch, is not native to but naturalized in Austin and used in many butterfly gardens.

Monarch caterpillars feeding on the leaves of a Tropical milkweed or Butterflyweed.

Chrysalis or Cocoon?

■ What's the difference between a chrysalis and a cocoon? Both are protective coverings for a pupa, or the stage between the larva (caterpillar) and adult (butterfly or moth) forms. A chrysalis, from the Latin meaning "gold," is the pupal stage of butterflies. The term is derived from the often metallic-like coloration found in the pupae of many butterflies. Chrysalides are often formed in the open and are usually attached to a surface by a combination of a silken pad spun by the caterpillar and a set of hooks at the tip of its abdomen. A cocoon is a silk case spun around the pupa of moths (and sometimes other insects). Cocoons may be soft or tough, opaque or translucent, and that depends on the type of insect larvae that produces it. Some larvae attach small twigs or pieces of vegetation to the outside of their cocoon to camouflage it, while others spin their cocoon in a concealed location, like the underside of a leaf or in a crevice, to protect themselves from predators.

of native plants. If they survive the winter, they will begin the trip back to Canada in late March or early April. Although the same butterflies that winter in Mexico don't survive long enough to see Canada once more, the next three generations carry on the lifecycle as they migrate north. Each first through third generation lives only six to eight weeks, and it is this fourth generation—the great, great grandchildren—that complete the return journey through Austin and back into Mexico.

Driven by seasonal changes such as temperature and day length, the migration of the Monarch is unique in the world. They travel up to a total of 3,000 miles—much farther than all other tropical butterflies—and they are the only butterfly species to make such a long, two-way migration every year. Amazingly, they fly in masses to the same winter roosts, often to the exact same trees, but unlike other migrating species such as birds and whales, it is their children's grandchildren that return south the following fall. Now that you know a little something about their magical migration, stop to admire these amazing beauties as you see them flutter by you this fall on their way to their winter home in Mexico.

WHERE TO WATCH:

❖ Usually in mid-October, you will begin to notice many more Monarch butterflies as they make their way south across Austin and Central Texas en route to their winter homes in the mountains of Mexico. Don't confuse them with American Snouts (*Libytheana carinenta*), a smaller dark brown and orange butterfly that often emerges and wanders in large numbers a few weeks after a fall rain.

❖ Plant native species of milkweeds in your yard and become a citizen scientist by participating in Monarch Watch's Waystation Program, (www.monarch watch.org/waystations/), and learn to create, preserve, and protect Monarch habitats.

Fabulous Fall Grasses

Austin and the Central Texas region are home to many species of fall-blooming native grasses. These "warm season grasses," so-called because their growth period occurs during our hottest weather and their dormancy period occurs in winter, provide extremely valuable habitat for ground-nesting birds

Bushy Bluestem forms coppery spikes as the weather cools.

as well as many mammals. They can be very deep-rooted, making for a long-lasting, stress-tolerant, low maintenance, erosion-controlling plant.

The root biomass of native warm season grasses far exceeds that of the introduced, non-native turf grasses, which enables these plants to increase the organic matter in our soils and allow for more rapid water infiltration rates, both of which are beneficial to soil and water quality. In addition, these native grasses tend to grow in bunches, which naturally allows the inclusion of native forbs, wildflowers, and legumes to further improve the quality of wildlife habitat through species biodiversity.

Aside from being highly deer-resistant, native grasses all provide seed for winter birds and are larval host plants for the skipper family of butterflies. Their foliage is used by birds and mammals for nesting material, and they can be very effective at controlling erosion and helping to build soil on steep slopes that are common in Central Texas.

Growing 2 to 5 feet tall, Bushy Bluestem (*Andropogon glomeratus*) prefers

The slender blue-green stems of Little Bluestem begin turning mahogany-red in September and remain all winter.

The large, graceful seedheads of Inland Sea Oats turn bright gold in the fall.

the moist soil of a wetland area, and its showy fall blooms on coppery-red stems resemble tufts of cotton candy. Slightly smaller at 2 to 3 feet tall, Little Bluestem (*Schizachyrium scoparium* var. *scoparium*) grows in drier areas with sun or part-shade, its blue-green foliage in summer turning mahogany-red with white tufts of blooms in the fall.

Inland Sea Oats (*Chasmanthium latifolium*), also known as Indian wood oats, wild oats, and river oats, is a perennial, clump-forming grass, 2–4 feet high, native to East and Central Texas. Its blue-green leaves turn yellow-gold in the fall, and give rise to oat-like flower spikelets from slender, arching branches. Found along watercourses, on shaded slopes, and in low thickets, it is the larval host plant for the group of butterflies known as the roadside-skippers.

Occuring mainly in sunny, well-drained areas like the limestone uplands near streams, Lindheimer's Muhly (*Muhlenbergia lindheimeri*) is a 2 to 5 foot grass with silvery seed heads that is an excellent soft-textured substitute for non-native pampas grass. The hill country version of Gulf Muhly, Seep Muhly (*Muhlenbergia reverchonii*) grows about 2 feet tall on grassy limestone slopes in dense tufts of slender stems and curled foliage, with a frothy pink bloom in the fall.

Sideoats Grama (*Bouteloua curtipendula* var. *curtipendula*), the state grass

In autumn, the lacy silver seedheads of Lindheimer's (Big) Muhly decorate the landscape.

of Texas, is not choosy about soils and at 2 to 3 feet is a good companion for wildflowers. Purplish, oat-like spikelets uniformly line one side of the stem, bleaching to a tan color in the fall. Staying low most of the year at 2 feet then getting tall before blooming in October, Yellow Indiangrass (*Sorghastrum nutans*) sports a plume-like seed head up to 6 feet tall, made up of gold and purplish-red sprays of small flowers and seeds. Like Bushy Bluestem and Little Bluestem, it is an important component species in the tallgrass prairie.

Seep Muhly sends up its frothy, purplish seed heads from a dense, curly base.

Oak-like spikelets line one side of the stem of Sideoats Grama, the state grass of Texas.

Now is the time to consider planting some of these warm season grasses on your property. They require little (if any) water or fertilizer after planting, and not only will they provide food and shelter for our native wildlife, but their showy seed heads will hold well into winter, adding movement, texture, and color to your wildscape.

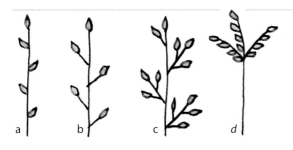

Different types of seed heads (inflorescence) can aid in proper identification of grasses: spike (a), raceme (b), panicle (c), and digitate spicate (d).

Nolinas

■ Close kin to yuccas and sotols and in the Agave family, nolinas are native evergreen plants that are frequently mistaken for grasses. Sacahuista, Basket Grass, or Beargrass (*Nolina texana*) is a 2-foot square clump of long, thin, rounded blades with one flat side often found on well-drained, dry slopes from part shade to full sun. It is common throughout the Edwards Plateau as well as in the Rio Grande plains and the Trans-Pecos regions. The similar-looking Devil's Shoestring or Ribbon Grass (*Nolina lindheimeriana*) is found only on the Edwards Plateau, and has long, flat blades with fine, saw-toothed edges. Its species name recognizes Ferdinand Lindheimer, an accomplished German botanist who studied Texas flora in the mid-nineteenth century.

▲ Nolina texana *is also called Sacahuista, from the Aztec meaning "thorn grass."*

◄ Nolina lindheimeriana *is also called Devil's Shoestring or Ribbon Grass, due to its long, flat, narrow leaves.*

WHERE TO WATCH:

❖ Bushy Bluestem and Yellow Indiangrass are typically found on moist, bottomland sites in deep soil, whereas Inland Sea Oats and Lindheimer's Muhly are found in woodland areas along streams.

❖ Little Bluestem prefers dry hills and forest borders, whereas Seep Muhly and Sideoats Gramma thrive on open, rocky slopes.

A River of Raptors

One of the most dramatic natural events occurs every fall when changing weather patterns mark the migration of hawks (also called raptors, or birds of prey) from their summer nesting and breeding grounds to their wintering grounds in South America. Northward migration in the spring months is more sporadic and allows for hawks to spread out over a larger geographic area. Fall migration is the more spectacular of the two, with millions of hawks observed overhead in concentrated groups within a period of only a few months.

Scientists believe that hawks use a myriad of tools to find their way along migratory routes. First and foremost, they orient themselves by using a sun compass, or knowing where the sun should be at any given time of day. Some also use a polarization pattern of light for orientation, and are able to find the portion of the sky where light is uni-directional and utilize it to estimate the sun's position. Lastly, most hawks bring into play a magnetic compass, which allows them to orient themselves to the Earth's magnetic field.

In order to get airborne and use these internal orientation systems, hawks find thermals, or large columns of warm air, and ride these rising air currents in a spiral, high into the sky. From this vantage point, they glide slowly down in the intended direction, and search for the next thermal to help move them along their way. From these elevated perspectives, hawks generally navigate by large geographic features or landmarks, such as coastlines, waterways, and mountain ranges.

The most common species of hawk that migrate over our area start with the Mississippi Kite (*Ictinia mississippiensis*), continue with the Broad-winged Hawk (*Buteo platypterus*), and end with Swainson's Hawk (*Buteo swainsoni*). Dark gray above and pale gray below with a red eye, long pointed wings, and a dark flared tail, the Mississippi Kite hunts primarily insects, eats on the wing, and nests in loose colonies in woodlands and swamps in the Southeast and

South-central United States. Brown-gray above with white underwings bordered in black, and a broad tail with black and white bands, the Broad-winged Hawk breeds in the eastern woodlands of the United States and Southern Canada. The largest of the three, the Swainson's Hawk light morph is the color form that is most likely seen in our area. In flight, their long, narrow pointed wings exhibit a dark trailing edge and light leading edge, a dark chest bib, and light face and lower belly. These hawks hunt chiefly small mammals and insects in the grassland areas of the Western United States and Canada.

Large groups of hawks flying and circling overhead are called "kettles" (as are large groups of a few other bird species who behave similarly). During fall migration, single kettles of 10,000 hawks are routine, and single flights of 100,000 hawks or more have been recorded. Occasionally, a strong cold front will ground several thousand hawks for the day and result in an overnight roost. Weather in the Northern and Eastern United States is one of the biggest factors in determining the timing of these migratory flights.

▲ *Broad-winged Hawks like this one, group together to migrate in the fall.*

▶ *On the way to its wintering grounds in Argentina, a Swainson's Hawk can travel over 120 miles per day.*

Hawkwatch

■ The Hawk Migration Association of North America defines a hawkwatch as "a systematic and organized effort to collect standardized migration count data about diurnal raptors." Observations are repeated (daily or almost daily) at an established site to gather information such as types of species, numbers present, migration behavior, and weather conditions. One such site in our area is the Hornsby Bend Bird Observatory (www.hornsbybend.org/hawkwatch-current.html), which regularly reports raptors such as Swainson's Hawks, Mississippi Kites, and Broad-winged Hawks during migration.

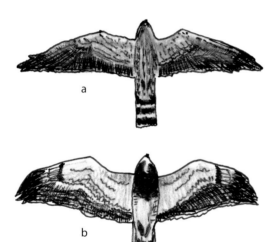

Migrating raptors, as viewed from below (not to scale): Mississippi Kite (a), Swainson's Hawk (b), and Broad-winged Hawk (c).

It was late into the nineteenth century before hawk migration was beginning to be understood. With large populations of hawks continuing to shift from breeding to wintering habitat, migration is a seasonal and predicable event that can be enjoyed and studied year after year.

WHERE TO WATCH:

❖ Join the Hawkwatch at Hornsby Bend, where you can view migrating raptors and learn from other interested and knowledgeable volunteers.

❖ Scan the skies as you drive around town this time of year, and you should notice more hawks overhead, often flying in groups or "kettles."

170 *October*

A resident Red-tailed Hawk (Buteo jamaicensis) *watches vigilantly over its territory.*

Blooming Mist

All members of the Aster family, the *Eupatorium* genus of flowering plants are characterized by their medium-tall to tall stems and triangular, toothed leaves, topped with a cluster of small composite flowers. They grab our attention in the fall as their blooms are prolific, like small clouds of mist, on which late-season butterflies, bees, and moths are eager to gather. It's easy to see why they are commonly called mistflowers, but they are also called bonesets, thoroughworts, and snakeroots.

To add to the mystery, the classification of this tribe of plants is the subject of ongoing research, and many species that were once grouped under *Eupatorium* have recently been moved to other plant families, or genera. *Conoclinium,* the mistflowers, is a genus that includes only four species, native to North America, and having blue to purple flowers. *Ageratina,* or snakeroots, has over 250 species, and they grow mainly in warmer regions.

October

Commonly named for medicinal uses, various members of this plant family have been used to treat fevers and other health ailments. Boneset alludes to the use of the plant to stimulate calcium production to speed the healing of broken bones, although the name may have also come from its use to treat dengue fever, also called breakbone fever due to the pain it inflicts. Thoroughwort is named for its "perfoliate" leaves, or the way the stem appears to pierce or go through the leaf.

In the Hill Country, Blue Mistflower (*Conoclinium coelestinum*) is also called Wild Ageratum or Blue Boneset. Forming fairly large, bushy clumps 1 to 4 feet tall on moist soils near streams and in low meadows, its opposite leaves are triangular, wrinkled, somewhat thick, and smell a bit like tomato plants when crushed. It prefers sun to partial shade, and its lavender to sky-blue clusters of flowers bloom from July to late November.

Also called Havana Snakeroot, White Mistflower, and White Shrub Mistflower, Shrubby Boneset (*Ageratina havanensis*) is a rounded, open woody shrub, 2 to 5 feet tall, and multi-branched. Its leaves are triangular with toothed edges, relatively thin, and about 2 inches long. Blooming in October and

Blue Mistflowers attract many species of bees and butterflies in the fall.

Mistflower leaves: Blue Mistflower (a), Gregg's Mistflower (b), Shrubby Boneset (c), and Late Boneset (d).

November, the profuse flowers are fuzzy, pinkish-white, and very fragrant. Deciduous and drought-tolerant, Shrubby Boneset is found on rocky hillsides and bluffs in the southern half of the Hill Country. Butterflies, moths, and hummingbirds, love the upright, fuzzy flower heads, and this plant is the larval

Shrubby Boneset blooms best when cut back severely each winter.

host plant for the difficult to identify butterfly, Rawson's Metalmark (*Calephelis rawsoni*).

Late Boneset (*Eupatorium serotinum*), also called Late-flowering Thorough-wort or White Boneset, is an open but erect woody shrub up to 3 feet tall, with leaves up to 5 inches long, opposite and coarsely toothed. Blooming in October and November, it likes partial shade, and is found in the eastern to central portion of the state, usually in meadows, woodland edges, near ponds or moist stream banks.

Regardless of their classification, these native fall bloomers are a haven for wildlife. Seek them out when hiking along your favorite trail—their intricate, fuzzy blooms beckon you to explore them up close and personal.

WHERE TO WATCH:

❖ Visit places like the Zilker and Natural Gardener butterfly gardens and the Lady Bird Johnson Wildflower Center to see mistflowers in bloom, and in the wild, find them on the shady hillsides in Bull Creek and Barton Creek greenbelts.

Gregg's Mistflower

◼ Named after the nineteenth century explorer and naturalist Josiah Gregg, Gregg's Mistflower (*Conoclinium greggii*) is native to West Texas but spreading eastward to the Edwards Plateau. Also called Palmleaf Thoroughwort or Purple Palmleaf Mistflower, this 1½ to 2 foot tall perennial has puffy, purple-blue flower heads from March through November. Often attracting impressive numbers of nectaring Queen butterflies in the fall, this plant is found along seasonally flooded streambeds and has a lighter green, more delicate foliage.

A Queen butterfly nectars on one of its favorite foodplants, a Gregg's Mistflower.

Fall-blooming White or Late Boneset is largely unbranched below, forming side stems near the apex.

Virginia Creeper (Parthenocissus quinquefolia) *is one of the earliest vines to show its autumn hues.*

CLIMATIC DATA FOR THE MONTH OF NOVEMBER IN AUSTIN.

	November 1	November 7	November 14	November 21	November 28
Record High	88°F	89°F	89°F	89°F	89°F
Average High	75°F	73°F	70°F	68°F	66°F
Average Low	54°F	52°F	50°F	47°F	46°F
Record Low	34°F	28°F	26°F	30°F	26°F
Sunrise	7:45 a.m.	6:50 a.m.	6:56 a.m.	7:02 a.m.	7:07 a.m.
Sunset	6:43 p.m.	5:39 p.m.	5:35 p.m.	5:32 p.m.	5:30 p.m.
Daylight	10 hr 58 min	10 hr 49 min	10 hr 39 min	10 hr 30 min	10 hr 23 min

Average Monthly Precipitation—2.51 inches

November

Leafy Treasures

Fall is the time when the quiet, green palette of summer gives way to the crisp reds, vibrant oranges, and mellow yellows that paint the natural landscape. During the growing seasons of spring and summer, our trees and shrubs use sunlight to convert water and carbon dioxide from the air into sugar. Called photosynthesis, this process begins to wane in November in Central Texas, and the leaves on some plants begin to change color in preparation for winter's rest.

Pigments are natural substances formed by the cells of leaves which provide the basis for leaf color. Most familiar is chlorophyll, which produces the color green, and is vitally important because it is required for photosynthesis. Carotenoids, which produce the colors yellow, orange, and brown, are common pigments in many fruits and vegetables, as are anthocyanins, which produce the color red. Both chlorophyll and carotenoids are present at the same time in leaf cells, but the chlorophyll covers the carotenoids and hence the leaves appear green in the spring and summer. Not all trees can make anthocyanins, however, and most are produced under specific conditions and only in the fall.

As the days grow shorter, the decreasing amount of sunlight eventually causes trees to stop producing chlorophyll. When this happens, the carotenoids in a leaf can finally show through, turning the leaves into a myriad of yellows, oranges, and browns. Red, on the other hand, is an entirely different matter. Affected by temperature and cloud cover, red fall colors can vary greatly from year to year. A lively showing of reds depends upon warm, sunny autumn days and cool, but not cold autumn nights. This type of weather pattern triggers the production of anthocyanins, which the tree produces as a form of protection. Anthocyanins allow trees to recover any sugar or nutrients left in the leaves, moving them through the leaf veins and down into the branches and trunk, and its presence generates the red color before the leaves fall off. Rainfall during the year can also affect fall color, with too much reducing the overall color intensity, and too little delaying the arrival of color.

Fall leaf color can easily be used to help identify local tree and shrub species, as they dot the hillsides, roadsides, and upper reaches of wooded canyons, contrasting well with the surrounding greens of Ashe Junipers and Live Oaks. Given a typical year of weather conditions and patterns, fall color begins in late October with the golden yellows of Cedar Elms (*Ulmus crassifolia*) and pale yellows of Eastern Cottonwoods (*Populus deltoides*), the color of which transforms the low-lying areas near creeks and streams. In November, the real show starts, with the bright yellow-oranges of Escarpment Black Cherries (*Prunus serotina* var. *eximia*), the deep reds, maroons, and orange-browns of Texas Red (Spanish) Oaks (*Quercus buckleyi*), and finishing with the brilliant orange-red foliage of the aptly named Flameleaf Sumac (*Rhus lanceolata*).

A typical fall landscape in the hills around Austin.

Oak Galls

▦ Most commonly found on oak trees, galls are round, highly distinctive but abnormal outgrowths of plant tissue usually caused by insects. Formation of a gall begins with the hatching of the eggs of certain wasp or fly species laid on the plant and the resulting larvae (or the adult females themselves) inject chemicals into the plant. The tissue swells in reaction and forms a microhabitat surrounding the larvae, providing them with nutrients and a safe place from predators. Once grown, the insects bore an exit hole in the gall and disperse. Gall-inducing insects are usually species-specific and sometimes even tissue-specific (branches, leaves, buds) in the plants they select. While

usually forming in the spring when most plant cell-division occurs, galls initially appear light green in color but become even more noticeable in the fall when oak trees drop their leaves. Dull, dry, and brown, the spent galls are often scavenged by mammals searching for leftover food as winter approaches.

An oak gall against a backdrop of fall foliage.

A tree's trunk and branches can survive the colder winter temperatures, but many leaves cannot. Made up of cells filled with water and sap, these tissues are unable to live through the winter, and the tree must shed them to ensure its survival. As the days grow shorter, the veins that carry sap to the rest of the tree eventually close. A separation layer forms at the base of each leaf stem, and when complete, the leaf falls. An exception is some oak species in which this layer never fully detaches and the dead leaves remain on the tree until new spring growth pushes them off to the ground. Once on the ground, the leaves slowly decompose with the help of earthworms, beneficial bacteria, and fungi, creating the soil necessary for the continuation of the cycle of life.

WHERE TO WATCH:

❖ Contrasting with the greens of Ashe Junipers and Live Oaks, bright splashes of fall color can be found all around us, in the native trees that cover the hills, define the canyon bottoms, and line many of the roads in the Austin area.

*As the temperatures drop, Mexican Buckeyes (*Ungnadia speciosa*) turn a golden yellow.*

A Texas Red Oak shows its brilliance against a blue autumn sky.

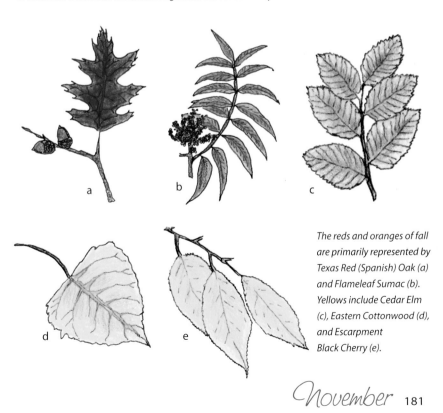

The reds and oranges of fall are primarily represented by Texas Red (Spanish) Oak (a) and Flameleaf Sumac (b). Yellows include Cedar Elm (c), Eastern Cottonwood (d), and Escarpment Black Cherry (e).

The Simple Beauty of Sparrows

Coming from the Anglo-Saxon word *spearwa* and literally meaning "flut-terer," sparrows often conjure up images of the ubiquitous and non-native House Sparrow (*Passer domesticus*) and the native House Finch (*Carpodacus mexicanus*), which isn't even a sparrow at all. While most sparrows are generally small to medium brown birds with streaks, the differences between sparrows can best be determined by their relative size, head markings, and habitat.

All sparrows have conical bills that they use to shell seeds, a primary component of their diet year-round, but especially in the winter months. There is little difference between the males and the females in terms of appearance, but males are larger than females. As a group, most sparrows are birds of

Chipping Sparrows are a slender sparrow with a rufous-tinged crown in winter that usually feed on the ground and travel in loose groups.

The fine streaks on its buffy breast and overall grayish-brown coloring help to identify this Lincoln's Sparrow.

Unlike the White-crowned Sparrow, the White-throated Sparrow (Zonotrichia albicollis) has both a black and white striped crown and a white throat, along with a bright yellow spot or "lore" between the eye and the bill.

The Field Sparrow (Spizella pusilla) often flies to the top of seed stalks and lets its weight carry the stems to the ground, where it begins to remove the seeds.

The Rufous-crowned Sparrow (Aimophila ruficeps) is a medium-sized sparrow with a rufous crown and a thick, black moustache or "malar" stripe.

grasslands, prairies, and marshes, and seem to prefer weedy fields and wood-land edges in the winter. Of the sparrow species that migrate, none travel further than the Southern United States or Northern Mexico.

One of our most common winter sparrows is the Chipping Sparrow (*Spizella passerina*). Small and slim, with a long notched tail, rusty cap, white stripe over the eye and a black line through the eye, this sparrow moves in loose flocks and frequently feeds in short grass and open woods. While still fairly abundant, this sparrow is declining in numbers, mainly due to habitat destruction, and winters in the southern part of the United States. When first identified in 1810 by American ornithologist Alexander Wilson, it was nick-named the "Social Sparrow" because it was easily approached and associated with human habitation.

A fairly large sparrow, the White-crowned Sparrow (*Zonotrichia leucophrys*) is distinguished by its black and white striped head, unmarked gray breast, and dark pink bill. It is found in large groups in thickets and weedy areas, foraging on the ground. Discovered in 1772 by German naturalist Johann Reinhold Forster, this sparrow was originally named the "White-eyebrowed Bunting," since in the Old World, sparrows were usually called buntings.

Found in a variety of grassy habitats, and often in small flocks, is the Savannah Sparrow (*Passerculus sandwichensis*). Streaked on both their backs and breasts, Savannah's have pink legs, yellow above the eye, a thin white median crown stripe, and a short notched tail. First described by British ornithologist John Latham in 1790, it was called a "Sandwich Bunting" because the first specimens were collected from Sandwich Bay in the Aleutian Islands of Alaska.

Lincoln's Sparrow (*Melospiza lincolnii*) is a medium-sized bird with a rather short tail, broad gray stripe above the eye, buffy moustache stripe, and a buffy upper breast with crisp, blackish streaks. Found in winter in brushy edges of ponds and other moist areas, this sparrow was named by John James Audubon in 1833 after his research companion, Thomas Lincoln, shot the first specimen in the Canadian province of Labrador.

Sparrows are gregarious and are often our most hardy winter visitors. Adorned in various shades of brown, gray, black, and white, they reflect the subdued hues of a winter landscape. Often dismissed as "little brown birds" when seen with the naked eye, these birds invite closer inspection and are nature's way of reminding us that subtle colors and patterns can be beautiful as well.

WHERE TO WATCH:

❖ Check out the bird blind at Pedernales State Park, for a close-up look at numerous wintering sparrows.

❖ Balcones Canyonlands National Wildlife Refuge, Reimer's Ranch, Platt Lane near Hornsby Bend, and the rural roads and fields surrounding Decker Lake are good places for observing sparrows.

The Fungus Among Us

Frequently upstaged by the brightly colored autumn leaves and hidden among the leaf litter on the forest floor are several types of interesting fungi. Fungi are separated from the plant kingdom because they do not contain chlorophyll, and do not make their own food through photosynthesis. Instead, fungi obtain the nutrients they need by breaking down other organic matter and sometimes other plants. Mycology, from the Greek *mycos* meaning "fungus," is the branch of biology dedicated to the study of these organisms, and is most often associated with mushrooms. Although mushrooms are the most well-known, some of the more interesting fungi that occur in the fall after sufficient rains include Puffballs, Earthstars, Earthballs, and Bird's Nests. These forms are

November

An Earthball with its outer skin split, showing mature purple-black spores.

grouped based on the shape of their fruiting body, or structure that produces the spores needed for reproduction.

Puffballs (*Lycoperdon pyriforme* and *perlatum*) and Earthstars (*Geastrum saccatum*) are characterized by fruiting bodies that look like a small ball. Unlike a mushroom, they have no stalk, and are normally found growing on wood or directly on the ground. They can range in size from small marbles to baseballs,

with the spores produced inside. Once mature, the spongy inside darkens and dries to a fine powder, and the spores are emitted out of a hole on top of the ball. Often found around the drip line of trees, this strategic placement serves the dual purpose of providing sufficient moisture until they are grown as well as sufficient force from the water droplets to act as a dispersal agent for the spores. When one translates the genus from Greek to English, *lyco* meaning "wolf" and *perdon* meaning "to break wind," it isn't hard to guess that a former common name for a Puffball was Wolf-fart! With a somewhat less flamboyant name but a more elaborate display, Earthstars get their common name from their thicker outer membrane, which when fully developed splits into rays that curve backward to form a distinctly star-like structure.

Earthballs (*Astraeus hygrometricus*) are often found wholly or partly underground, and have a fruiting body that simulates a ball with a thick, rind-like skin. Their spores are produced in the center of the ball, but unlike Earthstars, they are extruded not via a pore at the top but when the entire inner spore sac splits open. Often called a "False Earthstar" the outer rind of this fungus splits into seven to fifteen pointed rays that open when it rains or when humidity is high, and close again during drier periods. This repeated action relates to its species name, as if it were nature's hygrometer, measuring the changes in humidity.

November

A cluster of False Earthstars, opened and revealing their spent inner spore sacs.

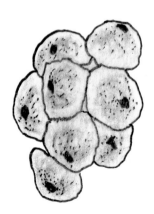

Puffballs are normally seen growing in groups.

Bird's Nests (*Cyathus stercoreus*) are fungi that have fruiting bodies resembling clusters of very small cup-shaped structures filled with tiny eggs. *Stercoreus* literally means "growing on dung," and that is where you are most likely to find this fungus. Also commonly found on woody mulch, each cup is only large enough to hold a drop of water, and the egg-like structures which contain the spores, are delicately attached to the cup by a finely coiled thread. When splashed out of the cup by raindrops, this thread-like structure uncoils, catches on to a chip of wood, blade of grass, or other organic matter, and splits open to release the spores inside.

The cup-shaped Bird's Nest Fungus contains small, flattened spheres resembling eggs.

Nostoc

■ A genus of freshwater cynobacteria or blue-green algae, *Nostoc* is often found on the ground in gravelly limestone areas. When dry, it is often overlooked, appearing brittle and black, but after a rain swells up into a conspicuous, green, jelly-like mass. Because of this physical transformation, some popular names for *Nostoc* are Star Jelly, Witches Butter, and Rot of the Stars. Because they contain protein and vitamin C, many *Nostoc* species are cultivated and produced for food, primarily in Asia, where is it called Fat Choy. However, research conducted at the Chinese University of Hong Kong showed that some species contain a toxic amino acid that can affect the normal function of nerve cells, and if ingested might lead to degenerative nerve diseases such as Alzheimer's, Parkinson's, and dementia.

A small colony of Nostoc *exhibiting its green, gelatinous mass.*

The next time you take a walk in the woods to admire the colors and changes that define the fall, don't forget to look down at your feet, where you can discover the smaller mysteries of the forest and appreciate their beauty from the ground up.

WHERE TO WATCH:

❖ Various species of Earthstars and Puffballs can often be found under the drip lines of oak trees, along the edges damp trails, and in the mossy, needle-strewn beds under Ashe Juniper trees.

❖ After a rain, look closely on the surface of your backyard mulch for small colonies of Bird's Nest fungus.

First Frost

Accompanying the crunching of fallen leaves and the rattling of seed pods drying in the breeze is the arrival of the first frost. This marks the seasonal change from our relatively warm autumn to the cooler days of a mild Central Texas winter. How does frost, this sparkling layer that sometimes covers the fall landscape, form?

When the temperature of the air reaches a point where the water vapor it contains can condense into water, it is called the dew point. The frost point is when the dew point falls below freezing, and rather than producing dew, it creates frost. Consisting of tiny, spike-like crystal structures (spicules) that grow out from a solid surface, frost generally forms on surfaces that are colder than the surrounding air. Even the size of the crystals can vary, depending upon the amount of time they took to grow, the relative changes in temperature, and the amount of water vapor available.

Cold air is denser than warm air, so quite often lower areas become colder

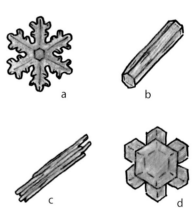

Shapes of frost crystals are determined by the temperature and humidity when formed. As temperature decreases, some commonly formed shapes include dendrites (a), columns (b), needles (c), and plates (d).

on calm nights due to differences in elevation. Known as surface temperature inversion, this phenomenon forms "frost pockets" or areas where frost forms first, due to cold air trapped against the ground. It is here, in these areas, that you can find a surprising but wonderful natural phenomenon called "frost flowers."

Many plants can be damaged or killed by freezing temperatures or frost, but this varies depending on the type of plant and tissue exposed to these conditions. In our area, there is a plant called Frostweed (*Verbesina virginica*), which is commonly found in low-lying areas near streams, creeks, canyon bottoms, and in dappled shade at woodland edges. Much of the year, Frostweed goes unnoticed while it grows tall and leafy, the top of each stalk crowned by a platter of small white flowers in the fall. With the first frost, the water contained in each plant stem expands, causing the stems to crack. Capillary action draws more water through the cracks, freezes when it hits the cold air, and forms long curls of ice like petals of a flower. These delicate flowers of the frost are fleeting in nature, and can only be found in early morning, since the rising temperature quickly melts them away.

Other plants have interesting seed-heads and seedpods at this time of year, providing a means for self-propagation as well as a winter source of food for wildlife. Goldenrods, Gayfeathers, Purple Coneflower, Maximillian Sunflower, Inland Sea Oats, and a few indigenous species of clematis are prime examples. Postpone cutting them to the ground until late winter, because each provides seeds that lend a helping hand to hungry critters and adds a distinct character to the landscape.

Our generally cool falls and temperate winters do not require most mammals to hibernate, but a few species of butterflies that emerge in the fall overwinter as adults. These butterflies have evolved to wait out the colder months in diapause, a physiological state of dormancy with unique triggering and releasing conditions. In the case of these butterflies, the first frost triggers their need to hide under tree bark or in a wood pile, venturing out only occasionally to bask in the sun on a warm winter day or take nourishment by feeding on the sap of a nearby tree. The increasing warmth in early spring releases these insects, ready to mate.

The most common overwintering butterflies in our area are the Question Mark (*Polygonia interrogationis*) and the Mourning Cloak (*Nymphalis antiopa*). Like other brushfoot butterflies in the Anglewing family, the Question Mark

Frostweed with a delicately formed and fleeting "frost flower."

The Question Mark butterfly is named for a silver mark on the underside of its hindwing which is broken into two parts: a curved line and a dot which form a ?-shape.

looks quite different depending on whether its wings are open or closed. While the upperside of the wings are colorfully marked with oranges, browns, and pinks, the undersides are a mosaic of drab browns, and along with their jagged edges, provide the perfect camouflage by mimicking a dead leaf. Mourning Cloaks, on the other hand, have a handsome purple-black upperside with a wide yellow outer margin with a row of iridescent blue spots on the inner edge of the border. Mourning Cloaks prefer the sap of oak trees, and they are known for walking down a tree trunk to the sap and feeding head downward.

On the surface, fall may seem as if nature is shutting down for the winter, but take the time for a second look. The first frost of the season is just another part of the ongoing cycle of life and renewal for our native plants and animals.

Dates of First Frost

■ Mid- to late November and early December are the times of year when we normally see our first frost. Clear skies, calm winds, and low humidity help the temperature to drop to the coldest levels since early spring. In Austin, the average date for a first freeze at Austin-Bergstrom International Airport (ABIA) is November 25th, while at Camp Mabry it occurs later, around December 2nd. Even though ABIA and Camp Mabry are not that far apart, ABIA is often 10 degrees colder because it is located near Onion Creek.

WHERE TO WATCH:

❖ In the early morning after a frost, look for frost flowers at the base of tall stalks of Frostweed in lower elevation drainages like those found in canyon bottoms and greenbelt areas along creeks and streams.

❖ On a calm, sunny winter day, overwintering brushfoot butterflies can sometimes be seen basking near their roosting sites in open woodlands and riparian areas with sap-producing trees such as willows, oaks, and cottonwoods.

The Red Admiral (Vanessa atalanta) *is yet another butterfly in the brush-footed family that is capable of overwintering.*

194 November

A female Goatweed Leafwing (Anaea Andria) *basks in the late autumn sun and prepares herself for winter.*

Western Scrub-Jays (Aphelocoma californica) *are found primarily west of the Balcones Escarpment.*

CLIMATIC DATA FOR THE MONTH OF DECEMBER IN AUSTIN.

	December 1	December 7	December 14	December 21	December 28
Record High	82°F	85°F	82°F	81°F	77°F
Average High	65°F	64°F	62°F	61°F	60°F
Average Low	45°F	43°F	42°F	41°F	40°F
Record Low	25°F	16°F	20°F	18°F	22°F
Sunrise	7:10 a.m.	7:14 a.m.	7:19 a.m.	7:23 a.m.	7:26 a.m.
Sunset	5:30 p.m.	5:30 p.m.	5:32 p.m.	5:35 p.m.	5:39 p.m.
Daylight	10 hr 20 min	10 hr 16 min	10 hr 13 min	10 hr 12 min	10 hr 13 min

Average Monthly Precipitation—2.47 inches

December

Common Myths of the Ashe Juniper

The Ashe Juniper (*Juniperus ashei*), more commonly but incorrectly known as the "cedar" tree, is not the bane of nature many people have come to believe. It is as much a part of the Texas Hill Country as wildflowers and limestone. The juniper tree can germinate on bare rock, quickly develop a thick canopy to protect the earth beneath it, and drop an enormous amount of leaf litter that can build soil and capture and hold water. Let's explore some of the common myths surrounding this tree, and in the process begin to appreciate its purpose, beauty, and wildness.

The typical form of a young Ashe Juniper.

Myth #1: The "cedar" tree is not a native tree.

While you have probably heard some of the tall tales about how junipers may have arrived in Central Texas, the undisputable proof that they are native lies in fossilized juniper pollen found in our area, dating back to the last Ice Age. Additionally, in historical records dating back to the late 1600s and early 1700s, junipers are accurately described by Spanish trailblazers, missionaries, and other early settlers and explorers alike. While native to our area, Ashe Junipers are invasive. Naturally occurring on steep, west-facing slopes, they have spread to cover most of our terrain due to our tendency to suppress the normal wildfires that kept them within their typical boundaries.

Myth #2: The "cedar" tree is a water hog.

Scientific stemflow studies have shown that the juniper does not take in much more water than any other native woody plant its size. Junipers are extremely drought tolerant, and their dense canopy breaks the impact of falling rain. This allows a thick organic litter to accumulate under the juniper, which slows down erosion and provides flash flood control. When slopes are clear-cut of juniper and native grasses cannot establish themselves, we not only lose our soil, but we may also be losing water. Eroded soil can fill the recharge cracks and limestone karsts with silt, which ultimately decreases the amount of water that percolates into the aquifer.

Myth #3: The "cedar" tree is a useless tree.

One of our endangered species, the Golden-cheeked Warbler, uses the soft bark strips of old-growth Ashe Junipers to build its nest. Many other species of wildlife use juniper thickets as escape cover and shelter, and in the winter, its berries feed several species of birds and mammals. Butterfly larvae, such as the Great Purple Hairstreak (*Atlides halesus*), Juniper Hairstreak (*Callophrys gryneus*), and the Tortricid or Leafroller moths, consume the foliage. And from a human point of view, oils provided by the juniper are used to scent perfumes and soaps, and the wood itself has been used for fuel, furniture, tools, fence posts, and just about everything in between.

Myth #4: Cutting down all the "cedar" trees in my yard will protect me from "cedar fever." ▶

The shaggy, old growth bark of a mature Ashe Juniper.

▶ December through March is the height of "cedar fever" season. This is the time of year that juniper trees (males only, the females produce the berries) produce copious amounts of pollen, up to several pounds per tree. Once this pollen becomes airborne, it travels hundreds of miles to reach every allergy sufferer. Face it, "cedar fever" is simply a natural part of living in Austin.

In short, the Ashe Juniper helps us to define what we call "a sense of place." Combined with the wild and tumbled terrain created by our ubiquitous limestone, the character of the juniper's twisted limbs and the smell of its foliage in the deep summer heat define the essence of the Texas Hill Country.

WHERE TO WATCH:

❖ Ashe Junipers are all around us, blanketing the hillsides and dotting the meadows in the Austin area, with old-growth trees over 30 feet tall, sporting shaggy bark, and larger trunk diameters.

❖ Learn more about the Ashe Juniper and sustainable gardening techniques at www.landsteward.net/mountain_cedar.html.

Nocturnal Neighbors

Who are some of those wild creatures of the night, inhabitants that dwell in the wildlands that surround us, living most of their lives in the dark?

Named for the nine bands that run across the armor plating on its back that give it protection and flexibility, the Nine-banded Armadillo (*Dasypus novemcinctus*) lives throughout most of the South-central and Southeastern

United States. It constructs burrows in loose Soil and Sometimes digs in lawns, flower beds, and under patios and decks in search of insects and other small invertebrates to eat. Mating occurs between July and August, but implantation is delayed until November, when a litter of four identical clones is delivered, their leathery skin pink until they mature to a grayish-brown. The Nine-banded Armadillo is the only armadillo that can "swim"—it can hold its breath as it walks across the bottom of flowing streams!

Recognized by its bandit mask and ringed tail, the Northern Raccoon (*Procyon lotor*) is a widespread mammal but not often seen due to its nocturnal habits. It consumes a highly varied diet, is very intelligent and curious, and possesses far greater manual dexterity than cats or dogs, enough to defeat any but the most determined defense of garbage cans or home gardens. Raccoons do not wash everything they eat, but they manipulate their food (appearing to wash it when water is available) in order to experience the object through touch rather than to actually clean it. They den above ground in tree cavities, chimneys and attics, underground in old burrows, storm sewers, and crawl spaces, and mate March to June with 3–5 young in each litter.

Another cat-sized carnivore with a long, raccoon-like tail, Ringtails (*Bassariscus astutus*) are almost wholly nocturnal and spend the majority of the day sleeping in their dens. With alternating black and white rings, their signature tail is bushy yet flattened and nearly as long as their head and body combined. They eat a wide variety of foods and leave their dens at night to feed. Ringtails live in many different habitats, but prefer rocky areas such as rock piles, stone fences, and canyon walls. Breeding in mid-spring, most litters consist of two to four young, which are born unable to see or hear, and are

The Northern Raccoon (a) and Ringtail (b) are closely related.

covered with short, pale hair. By the age of 4 months, young Ringtails have acquired their adult coloring.

More often smelled than seen is the Striped Skunk (*Mephitis mephitis*), whose primary defense is a complex substance that includes sulfuric acid and can be "fired" from either of its two independently targetable anal glands. Skunks tend to stand and face a threat, usually giving a warning by stomping up and down on their front feet, rather than trying to escape. They may dig their own burrows or use hollow logs or wood/rock piles for dens, and give birth in May to June to anywhere from three to ten young.

A Striped Skunk can be safely seen at the Austin Nature & Science Center.

Known to be native to and found throughout the United States, the Gray Fox (*Urocyon cinereoargenteus*) is primarily nocturnal when living around humans. Lacking the white tip at the end of their tail like Red Foxes, Gray Foxes can vary greatly in color and are described as "cat-like," due to the way they stalk their small prey. Being omnivores, they prefer to live in woodlands, and unlike the Red Fox, are capable of climbing trees. Using burrows and brush piles as dens, they give birth to four or five "kits" in March or April.

Having more teeth (50!) than any other North American mammal, the Virginia Opossum (*Didelphis*

Peaceful Coexistence

■ Learn how to peacefully coexist with our wild neighbors and resolve occasional human-animal conflicts around homes and buildings with the book *Wild Neighbors: The Humane Approach to Living with Wildlife* by The Humane Society of the United States. Should you find an injured wild creature, be sure to first check with Austin Wildlife Rescue (www .austinwildliferescue.org) or by calling their hotline at 512-472-WILD (9453) to determine what is the best approach for dealing with the situation at hand.

A member of the dog family, the Gray Fox is more cat-like and sometimes very curious.

The Virginia Opossum can feign death or "play possum" for up to four hours.

virginiana) is the only marsupial found north of Mexico. Their young are born in almost embryonic form, and make their way into a pouch where they are nourished and developed. Opossums live very short lives (only three years in the wild) with females living through only one breeding season and raising two litters with up to a dozen young in each. When confronted, they open their mouths to display their teeth, and may even hiss, but they'd rather not fight.

While most humans are asleep, these nighttime creatures go about their seemingly invisible lives. The more we know about our nocturnal neighbors, the better we can learn how to coexist peacefully with them and share the same natural environment.

WHERE TO WATCH:

- ❖ See a Northern Raccoon, Gray Fox, Striped Skunk, and other mammals up-close at the Austin Nature and Science Center and the Austin Zoo.
- ❖ Armadillos are often seen at dawn and dusk, digging in irrigated, suburban lawns for grubs and non-native flower bulbs to eat.
- ❖ Consider volunteering for Austin Wildlife Rescue (www.austinwildliferescue .org), where you could have the opportunity to care for and help rehabilitate raccoons, opossums, armadillos, and other mammals, as well as numerous birds and reptiles.

Fantastic Fossils

From the Latin *fossus,* literally meaning "having been dug up," fossils are the preserved remains or traces of animals, plants, and other organisms from the remote past. The study of fossils is called paleontology, a science that helps us understand how and when fossils were formed, as well as the evolutionary relationships between organisms, and has greatly contributed to our under-standing of ancient plants and animals and the natural world in which they lived.

Fossilization is an exceptionally rare occurrence, because most components of formerly living things tend to decompose relatively quickly following death. In order for an organism to be fossilized, the remains normally need to be covered by sediment as soon as possible. Exceptions to this condition are if an organism becomes frozen, desiccated (exposed to extreme dryness), or comes to rest in an oxygen-free environment. There are several different types of fossils and fossilization processes, but due to the combined effect of decomposition and simple mathematical chance, fossilization tends to favor organisms with hard body parts, those that were widespread, and those that lived for a long time.

The rocks of the Edwards Plateau consist primarily of Lower Cretaceous or Commanche Series limestones and chalks, formed over 100 million years ago, many of which are very fossiliferous. Part of the Mesozoic or "middle-life" geologic era, outcrops of these rocks and their associated fossils can be found along many streams, roads, and highways of Austin and surrounding areas. These fossils are usually abundant and varied, and most commonly those of invertebrates, or animals without a backbone or spinal column. This includes cephalopods (marine invertebrates with well-defined head and eyes and tentacles around the mouth such as squid, octopus, nautilus, and ammonites), pelecypods (bi-valved aquatic invertebrates such as clams and oysters), gastropods (terrestrial or aquatic invertebrates with a single-valved, coiled shell such as snails), and echinoids (bottom-dwelling, unattached marine invertebrates with an exoskeleton of plates covered by movable spines such as sea urchins).

Although Texas does not have a state fossil, it does have a fossil for its state stone, which is petrified palm wood. This wood is the petrified remains of trees

Natural History Resources

■ The Texas Natural Science Center in Austin is home to the Texas Memorial Museum (www.utexas.edu/tmm), which has exhibits and educational programs aimed to "encourage awareness and appreciation of the interplay of biological, geological, and environmental forces as they affect your world." Partnering with area schools, colleges/units of the University of Texas, and other informal science organizations, the museum houses 5.7 million specimens, many unique to Texas, and offers public events such as Family Fossil Fun Days and Identification Days that draw 10,000-plus visitors annually.

Austin Nature & Science Center (ANSC)

■ Part of the Parks & Recreation Department, the Austin Nature & Science Center (www.ci.austin.tx.us/ansc) is near Zilker Park and provides visitors with a living museum through interpretive exhibits, children's programs, hands-on collections, and short trails, with the goal of increasing knowledge, awareness, and appreciation of our natural environment.

With caution, roadcuts like this one on Loop 360, can be great places to search for fossils.

that grew on the Gulf coastal plain around 30 million years ago. At that time the shore of the Gulf of Mexico was further north than it is now, which explains why the wood is usually found in the more northern areas of the state, as well as in Louisiana and Mississippi. Of all the petrified wood found in Texas, petrified palm wood is the most common. Formed when a palm tree died and was buried by sediments, minerals in the groundwater permeated the wood, replacing the original organic matter and turning the wood to stone. The main

a

b

c

d

Common fossils of the Cretaceous Period: cephalopod (a) coiled in a single plane with shell divided by internal partitions; pelecypod (b) shells or valves similar to clams with plane of symmetry parallel to hinge; gastropod (c) coiled in a single plane with no internal shell partitions; and echinoid (d) disk or dome-shaped with a star pattern on top.

mineral that remains is silica, but trace elements in the silica impart a variety of colors to the petrified wood.

Simply put, the conditions under which fossilization takes place are quite rare, and it is highly unlikely that any given organism will leave behind a fossil. So when you come across a fossil as you explore Central Texas, it gives you even more reason to celebrate their mystique and fantastic beauty.

WHERE TO WATCH:

❖ While fossils can be observed and photographed in our parks, preserves, and greenbelts, they can only be collected in places like the road cuts along Highway 360.

❖ Visit the Texas Memorial Museum to view a large fossil collection on display, or trade for fossils at the Discovery Desk at the Austin Nature & Science Center (ANSC).

Silent Flight

One of the most unique adaptations in the natural world is the silent flight of

Even fossilized dinosaur tracks can be found in the Austin area.

owls. Their primary flight feathers have comb-like leading edges, which break down the turbulence created by air flowing over their wings and allow these birds to fly with great stealth.

The Barred Owl (*Strix varia*) goes by many other common names, but is probably best known as the "hoot owl," due to its call (*who cooks for you, who cooks for you all?*). This owl prefers to live in large blocks of forest, especially near water, and in our area is most often found near the Colorado River and its associated lakes and streams. The only typical owl in the Eastern United States with brown eyes instead of yellow, the Barred Owl has a pale face, dark rings around its eyes, and a yellow beak. Its head is round and lacks any ear tufts, and its body is a light gray-brown mottled by horizontal barring on its chest and lengthwise streaks on its belly.

A medium-sized owl at 17 to 19 inches tall with a wingspan 40 inches or more, the Barred Owl has been expanding its range westward in the last century. Like the Eastern Screech-Owl, its main predator is the Great Horned Owl, and although they often live in the same area, they will avoid having overlapping territories. They eat small mammals, birds, and invertebrates, as well as amphibians and reptiles, and frequently wade into water to catch crayfish, fish, and turtles. In fact, the belly feathers of some Barred Owls are tinged pink, most likely due to the amount of crayfish in their diet.

Barred Owls typically nest in cavities of deciduous trees, use open nests made by larger animals such as hawks, crows, or squirrels, and even human-made nest boxes. Although they are permanent residents, they may wander after the nesting season, often coming back the following year to reuse the same nesting site. In Central Texas, two to four eggs are laid in January, with hatching occurring in four weeks and the young fledging four to five weeks later. Hunting occurs largely at dusk and dawn, by waiting on a perch and swooping down on prey. Of all the owls in Texas, however, the Barred Owl is the one most likely to be active during the day, especially when hunting for food to feed hungry just-hatched chicks.

The most widely distributed owl in the world and the most widespread of all birds is the Barn Owl (*Tyto alba*). With a white or mostly white underside, lightly spotted breast, dark eyes and a heart-shaped, white face surrounded by a tawny halo, its scientific name literally means "white owl," but it is also known as ghost owl, death owl, and demon owl due to its pale appearance and eerily silent flight. Long legs, a round head with no ear tufts, and drawn-out, hissing scream for a call add to the image conjured up by its common names.

Barred Owls often fluff up their feathers to appear larger when faced with a perceived threat.

Owl Feather Structure

■ The structure of an owl's feather is the main reason they can fly so silently. The leading edge of their primary wing feathers are serrated like a comb, which breaks down the turbulence into smaller, micro-turbulences. The soft, tattered edges of their secondary feathers allow those small currents of air to pass through them and further reduce the turbulence behind their wings. In addition, the velvety down feathers found in the wing linings and on their legs also dampen and absorb sound frequencies. Together, these features allow the owl to greatly reduce the overall noise caused by the turbulence of air flowing over them as they fly. Coupled with the fact that some owls can rotate their heads 270 degrees, this design makes for a very fearsome predator.

a

b

Owl primary flight feathers (not to scale): Barred Owl (a), and Barn Owl (b).

Found in open habitats such as grasslands, marshes, and agricultural fields, the Barn Owl hunts at night by flying low over the ground, looking for small mammals. While it has excellent low-light vision, its ability to locate prey by sound alone sets it apart from any other animal species. At 12 to 15 inches in length and a wingspan of 40 to 50 inches, the Barn Owl is one of the few bird species where the female is showier than the male. Having a reddish chest marked by more numerous spots, those females that are heavily spotted appear to be more successful at mating, raising chicks, and resisting typical parasites and diseases.

Barn Owls can breed up to a few times per year, depending on the food supply. During courtship, both the male and the female screech, and the male will then conduct what is known as a "moth flight," where he hovers in front of the perched female with his long legs dangling, for several seconds. Barn Owl pairs typically remain together as long as both are alive. Their clutch size varies widely from 2–18 eggs, which are laid in nest cups made from shredded owl pellets. These owls use both human-made structures such as nest boxes and buildings, or natural cavities in trees and cliffs, for locating their nests.

WHERE TO WATCH:

❖ In the wild, Barred Owls can be heard and sometimes seen at dusk along the trails by the Colorado River at Hornsby Bend and nearby Platt Lane.
❖ The Austin Nature & Science Center offers close-up looks at both Barred and Barn owls.

A pair of Barn Owls are right at home at the Austin Nature & Science Center.

References

Here is a list of books and other reference material for use when learning about nature in Austin and surrounding areas.

Birds

Dunn, J. L., J. Alderfer. 2006. *National Geographic Field Guide to the Birds of North America.* Washington, D.C.: National Geographic Society.

Lockwood, M. W. 2001. *Birds of the Texas Hill Country.* Austin: University of Texas Press.

———and B. Freeman. 2004. *The Texas Ornithological Society Handbook of Texas Birds.* College Station: Texas A&M University Press.

Peterson, R. T. 2009. *Peterson Field Guide to Birds of North America.* New York: Houghton Mifflin Harcourt Publishing Company.

Travis Audubon Society. 2003. *Birds of the Austin Texas Region: A Seasonal Distribution Checklist.* Round Rock, Texas. http://www.travisaudubon.org/

Rylander, K. 2002. *The Behavior of Texas Birds.* Austin: University of Texas Press.

Sibley, D. A. 2000. *National Audubon Society The Sibley Guide to Birds.* New York: Alfred A. Knopf.

Wauer, R. H., M. A. Elwonger. 1998. *Birding Texas.* Guilford, Conn.: The Globe Pequot Press, Morris Book Publishing, L.L.C.

Mammals

Burt, W. H., R. P. Grossenheider. 1976. *A Field Guide to the Mammals of North America.* New York: Houghton Mifflin Company.

Bowers, N., R. Bowers, K. Kaufman. 2004. *Kaufman Focus Guide to Mammals of North America.* New York: Houghton Mifflin Company.

Elbroch, M. 2003. *Mammal Tracks & Sign: A Guide to North American Species.* Mechanicsburg, Penn.: Stackpole Books.

Hadidan, J., G. R. Hodge, J. W. Grandy. 1997. *Wild Neighbors: The Humane Approach to Living with Wildlife.* Washington, D.C.: Humane Society of the United States.

Schmidly, D. J. 2004. *The Mammals of Texas* (revised edition). Austin: University of Texas Press.

Tuttle, M. D. 2003. *Texas Bats.* Austin: University of Texas Press.

Reptiles and Amphibians

Bartlett, R. D., P. P. Bartlett. 1999. *A Field Guide to Texas Reptiles & Amphibians.* Houston: Gulf Publishing Company.

Dixon, J. R. 2000. *Amphibians and Reptiles of Texas*. College Station: Texas A&M University Press.

———and J. E. Werler. 2005. *Texas Snakes: A Field Guide*. Austin: University of Texas Press.

Price, A. H. 1998. *Poisonous Snakes of Texas*. Austin: Texas Parks and Wildlife Press.

Tennant, A. 1998. *A Field Guide to Texas Snakes*. Houston: Gulf Publishing Company.

Insects and Arachnids

Abbott, J. C. 2005. *Dragonflies and Damselflies of Texas and the South-Central United States*. Princeton, N. J.: Princeton University Press.

Brock, J. P., K. Kaufman 2003. *Kaufman Field Guide to the Butterflies of North America*. New York: Houghton Mifflin Company.

Capinera, J. L., R. D. Scott, T. J. Walker. 2004. *Field Guide to Grasshoppers, Katydids, and Crickets of the United States*. Ithaca, N.Y.: Cornell University Press.

Covell Jr., C. V. 2005. *A Field Guide to Moths of Eastern North America*. Martinsville, Va.: Virginia Museum of Natural History.

Drees, B. M., J. A. Jackman. 1998. *A Field Guide to Common Texas Insects*. Houston: Gulf Publishing.

Dunkle, S. W. 2000. *Dragonflies through Binoculars: A Field Guide to Dragonflies of North America*. New York: Oxford University Press.

Eaton, E. R., K. Kaufman. 2007. *Kaufman Field Guide to Insects of North America*. New York: Houghton Mifflin Company.

Evans, A. V. 2008. *National Wildlife Federation Field Guide to Insects and Spiders of North America*. New York: Sterling Publishing Company.

Glassberg, J. 1999. *Butterflies through Binoculars: The East*. New York: Oxford University Press.

Himmelman, J. 2002. *Discovering Moths: Nighttime Jewels in Your Own Backyard*. Camden, Maine: Down East Books.

Neck, R. W. 1996. *A Field Guide to Butterflies of Texas*. Houston: Gulf Publishing Company.

Paulson, D. 2009. *Dragonflies and Damselflies of the West*. Princeton, N. J.: Princeton University Press.

Powell, J. A., P. Opler. 2009. *Moths of Western North America*. Berkeley, Calif.: University of California Press.

Wagner, D. L. 2005. *Caterpillars of Eastern North America*. Princeton, N. J.: Princeton University Press.

Wauer, R. H. 2006. *Finding Butterflies in Texas: A Guide to the Best Sites*. Boulder, Colo.: Johnson Books, Big Earth Publishing.

Mollusks

Howells, R. G., R. W. Neck, H. D. Murray. 1996. *Freshwater Mussels of Texas*. Austin: University of Texas Press.

Astronomy

Pasachoff, J. M. 2000. *A Field Guide to Stars and Planets*. New York: Houghton Mifflin Company.

Geology

Finsley, C. E. 1999. *A Field Guide to Fossils of Texas*. Houston: Gulf Publishing.

Matthews III, W. H. 1992. *Texas Fossils: An Amateur Collector's Handbook*. Austin: University of Texas, Bureau of Economic Geology.

Pough, F. H. 1996. *A Field Guide to Rocks and Minerals*. New York: Houghton Mifflin Company.

Roberts, D. C. 1996. *A Field Guide to Geology: Eastern North America*. New York: Houghton Mifflin Company.

Trippet, A. R., L. E. Garner. 1992. *Guide to Points of Geologic Interest in Austin*. Austin: University of Texas, Bureau of Economic Geology.

Plants

Bender, K. 2009. *Texas Wildscapes, Gardening for Wildlife*. Austin: University of Texas Press.

Enquist, M. 1989. *Wildflowers of the Texas Hill Country*. Austin: Lone Star Botanical.

Loflin, B., S. Loflin. 2006. *Grasses of the Texas Hill Country*. College Station: Texas A&M University Press.

————. 2009. *Texas Cacti*. College Station: Texas A&M University Press.

Loughmiller, C., L. Loughmiller. 2006. *Texas Wildflowers: A Field Guide* (revised edition). Austin: University of Texas Press.

Lynch, Brother D. 1981. *Native & Naturalized Woody Plants of Austin & the Hill Country*. Austin: S.N. Publishing Company.

Metzler, S., V. Metzler. 1992. *Texas Mushrooms: A Field Guide*. Austin: University of Texas Press.

Poole, J. M., W. R. Carr, D. M. Price, J. R. Singhurst. 2007. *Rare Plants of Texas*. College Station: Texas A&M University Press.

Simpson, B. J. 1999. *A Field Guide to Texas Trees*. Houston: Gulf Publishing.

Tull, D., G. O. Miller. 1999. *A Field Guide to Wildflowers, Trees, & Shrubs of Texas*. Houston: Lone Star Books.

Turner, M. 2009. *Remarkable Plants of Texas*. Austin: University of Texas Press.

Vines, R. A. 1994. *Trees of Central Texas*. Austin: University of Texas Press.

Wrede, J. 2005. *Trees, Shrubs, and Vines of the Texas Hill Country*. College Station: Texas A&M University Press.

Balcones Canyonlands Preserve (BCP)

For BCP maps of some individual tracts:
www.ci.austin.tx.us/water/wildland/maps.htm

References 215

For BCP access information:
www.ci.austin.tx.us/water/wildland/bcpaccess.htm

Water Quality Protection Lands (WQPL)
For WQPL information:
www.ci.austin.tx.us/water/wildland/waterqualityprotectionland.htm

City of Austin Parks & Recreation Department
List of Parks:
www.ci.austin.tx.us/parks/parks.htm
List of Preserves:
www.ci.austin.tx.us/parks/preserves.htm

Other Important/Interesting Natural Areas to Visit:
Bastrop State Park (www.tpwd.state.tx.us/spdest/findadest/parks/bastrop/)
Blanco State Park (www.tpwd.state.tx.us/spdest/findadest/parks/blanco/)
Buescher State Park (www.tpwd.state.tx.us/spdest/findadest/parks/buescher/)
Canyon Lake (www.swf-wc.usace.army.mil/canyon/)
Canyon of the Eagles (www.canyonoftheeagles.com/)
Commons Ford Park (www.wildtexas.com/texas-parks/common-ford-park-lake-austin)
Granger Lake (www.swf-wc.usace.army.mil/granger/)
Guadalupe River State Park (www.tpwd.state.tx.us/spdest/findadest/parks/
     guadalupe_river/)
Hamilton Pool Nature Preserve (www.co.travis.tx.us/tnr/parks/hamilton_pool.asp)
Inks Lake State Park (www.tpwd.state.tx.us/spdest/findadest/parks/inks/)
Lake Buchanan (www.highlandlakes.com/lakebuchanan/)
Lake Georgetown (www.swf-wc.usace.army.mil/georgetown/)
McKinney Falls State Park (www.tpwd.state.tx.us/spdest/findadest/parks/
     mc_kinneyfalls/)
McKinney Roughs Nature Park (www.lcra.org/parks/developed_parks/mckinney_
     roughs.html)
Milton Reimers Ranch Park (www.co.travis.tx.us/tnr/parks/reimers_ranch.asp)
Pace Bend Park (www.co.travis.tx.us/tnr/parks/pace_bend.asp)
Palmetto State Park (www.tpwd.state.tx.us/spdest/findadest/parks/palmetto/)
Pedernales Falls State Park (www.tpwd.state.tx.us/spdest/findadest/parks/
     pedernales_falls/)
Westcave Preserve (www.westcave.org/)

Index

Note: Page numbers in *italics* indicate photographs and illustrations.

Index 219

caves and caverns (*cont.*)
and crickets, 143
and endangered species, xvii, 134
formation of, 103, *133*, 133–34
and salamanders, 97, 99
"show" caves, 135
species found in, 134–35
Cave Without a Name, 135
Cecropia Moth (*Hyalophora cecropia*),
150–51, *151*
Cedar Elm (*Ulmus crassifolia*), 178, *181*
The Cedar Lady Show (radio), 200
cedar trees, 197, 198–200. *See also* Ashe
Juniper (*Juniperus ashei*)
Cedar Waxwing (*Bombycilla cedrorum*),
1–2, *3*, 4
centipedes, *123*, 125, *125*
Central Flyway, 47, 158
cephalopods, 205, *206*
Chastetree, 72
cherry trees, *112*, 112–13, 178, *181*
Chimney Swift (*Chaetura pelagica*), 49
Chinaberry, 71
Chinese Photinia, 72
Chinese Tallow Tree, 71
Chipping Sparrow (*Spizella passerina*),
182, 184, *185*
Chiroptera, 32
chirping frogs, 59, 62, 63
chlorophyll, 177
chorus frogs, 59, *61*, 61–63
Christmas Cholla (*Cylindropuntia lepto-
caulis*), 40–41, *41*, *42*, 45
chrysalides, 160
Chuck-will's-widow (*Caprimulgus caro-
linensis*), 47
cicadas, *102*
Clammyweed (*Polanisia dodecandra*), 52
Clean Creek Challenge, 106
clematis, 191
Cliff Chirping Frog (*Syrrhophus marnockii*), *62*, 63

Cliff Swallow (*Petrochelidon pyrrhonota*),
48
climatic data
January, xxii
February, 14
March, 28
April, 47
May, 64
June, 84
July, 102
August, 120
September, 136
October, 156
November, 176
December, 196
Clubtail (*Gomphus militaris*), 111
coachwhip snakes, 138
Cochineal (*Dactylopius coccus*), 43, *43*
Cock's Comb (*Hexalectris spicata* var.
spicata), 95, *96*
cocoons, 160
collared-doves, 35, 37–38, *38*, 39
Colorado River, 58, 73, *74*, 97, 101, 103,
208, 211
comets, 121–22
Common Privet, 71
Commons Ford Park, 27
Common Snapping Turtle (*Chelydra
serpentina*), 116
Common Sunflower (*Helianthus an-
nuus*), 143
Congress Avenue Bridge, 33–34, 35
Conoclinium (mistflowers), 171–74, *172*,
173, *174*, *175*
conservation efforts, xv–xx, 33. *See also*
Balcones Canyonlands Conservation
Plan (BCCP); Balcones Canyonlands
Preserve (BCP)
Bat Conservation International, 33,
34
Grow Green Program, 78
habitat preservation, xvii–xviii

Index 221

geology. *See also* aquifers; caves and
  caverns
    fossils, xiv, 23, 204–7, *206, 207*
    limestone formations, xiii–xix, *xiv,
      xvi,* 45, 205
Giant Cane, 71
Giant Coralroot (*Hexalectris grandiflora*),
  95, *96*
Giant Lichen Orbweaver (*Araneus bicen-
  tenarius*), 86
Giant Ragweed (*Ambrosia trifida* var.
  texana), *143*
Giant Redheaded centipede (*Scolopendra
  heros* var. *castaneiceps*), 125, *125*
Giant Swallowtail butterfly (*Papilio
  cresphontes*), 50
Giant Walkingstick (*Megaphasma dentri-
  cus*), 145
Glen Rose Formation, xiv, *xiv*
glochids, 40
Goatweed Leafwing butterfly (*Anaea
  Andria*), *195*
Golden-cheeked Warbler (*Dendroica
  chrysoparia*), xv–xvii, *29,* 29–32, 55,
  198
Goldenrods, 191
Goldenwave (*Coreopsis* sp.), 52
grape vines, *113,* 114
grasses, 72, 161–68, *167*
grasshoppers, 141–42, *142*
Gray Fox (*Urocyon cinereoargenteus*), *7,*
  202, *203*
Gray Hairstreak butterfly (*Strymon
  melinus*), 67
Greater Scaup (*Aythya marila*), *13*
Great Horned Owl (*Bubo virginianus*),
  16–17, *17,* 208
Great Purple Hairstreak butterfly (*Atlides
  halesus*), 50, *64,* 198
Green Anole (*Anolis carolinensis*), 80–81,
  82
greenbelts, 68, 88, *106,* 194, 207

Green Lynx Spider (*Peucetia viridans*),
  128–29, 130, *130*
Green Neighbor Program, 106
green snakes, 139
Green Tree Frog (*Hyla cinerea*), *59,* 60,
  63
Gregg, Josiah, 174
Gregg's Mistflower (*Conoclinium greggii*),
  173, 174, *174*
Grooved Nipple Cactus (*Coryphantha
  sulcata*), 41, 45, *45*
Grow Green Program, 78
Guadalupe River, 58
Gulf Coast Toad (*Bufo valliceps valliceps*),
  89, 89–90, *90*
Gulf Fritillary butterfly (*Agraulis vanil-
  lae*), 94
Gulf Muhly (*Muhlenbergia reverchonii*),
  164, *166*

habitat preservation, xvii–xviii. *See also*
  environmental health
hairstreak butterflies, 50, *50, 64, 67,* 198
Halictid sweat bee, *76*
Halloween Pennant (*Celithemis eponina*),
  109, *110*
Hamilton Pool, 27
Havana Snakeroot (*Ageratina havanen-
  sis*), 172–73, *173*
Hawk Migration Association of North
  America, 170
Hawk Moths, 78, *79,* 150
hawks, 168–70, *169, 170, 171*
Hawkwatch, 170
Heavenly Bamboo, 71
Henry's Elfin butterfly (*Callophrys
  henrici*), 50
Hexalectris orchids, 95, *96*
Hill Country Rain Lily (*Cooperia pedun-
  culata*), 57–58
Holly Fern, 71
honeybees, *77*

Honey Mesquite (*Prosopis glandulosa* var. glandulosa), 47
honeysuckle, 2, 71, 146
Hoot Owl (*Strix varia*), 208
horned lizards, 83
horned owls, 16–17, *17*, 208
Hornsby Bend, 112, 118, 170, 185, 211
Hornsby Bend Bird Observatory (HBBO), 3, 13, 170
House Finch (*Carpodacus mexicanus*), 182
House Sparrow (*Passer domesticus*), 182
hummingbirds, 77–78, *79*, 146–49, *147*, *148*, 173
Hummingbirds of Texas (Shackelford, Lindsay, and Klym), 149

Imperial Moth (*Eacles imperialis*), 150
Inca dove (*Columbina inca*), 35, 36–37, *37*, 38, *39*
Indian Blanket (*Gaillardia pulchella*), 51, *51*, 52, *70*
Indiangrass, 165
Indian Paintbrush (*Castilleja indivisa*), 50
indicator species, 1, 62, 75, 92, 97, 109
Inland Sea Oats (*Chasmanthium latifolium*), *164*, 168, 191
Inner Space Caverns, 135
insects. *See also* butterflies; moths
  cochineal, 43, *43*
  crickets, 141, *142*, 142–43
  damselflies, 109, *110*
  dragonflies, 107–12, *108*, *110*
  katydids, 141, *142*, 144, *145*
  as pollinators, 49
  walkingsticks, 145
invasive species, xx, 68–72
ivy, 71

Japanese Honeysuckle, 71
Jewel Box Spider (*Gasteracantha cancriformis*), 128
Jimsonweed (*Datura stramonium*), 79

Johnson, Lyndon Baines, 51
Jollyville Plateau Salamander (*Eurycea tonkawae*), 97–100
Juniper Hairstreak butterfly (*Callophrys gryneus*), 50, *50*, 198
junipers, *14*. *See also* Ashe Juniper (*Juniperus ashei*)
  bark of, *199*
  berries of, *4*
  and Cedar Waxwings, *3*
  and Golden-cheeked Warblers, xvii, 29, 30–32
  myths about, 197–200
  typical form, *197*

karst features, xvii–xix, 31, 132, 198
karst invertebrates, xvii
katydids, 141, *142*, 144, *145*
kestrels, 1, 2, *3*, 4
kingbirds, 48, *48*, 52
kites, 168–69, 170, *170*
Kretschmarr Cave Mold Beetle, xvii
Kudzu, 71

Lace Cactus (*Echinocereus reichenbachii*), 41, *44*, 45
Lady Bird Johnson Wildflower Center
  birds, 4
  cacti, 45
  and edible fruits and berries, 114
  "Gardens on Tour," 80
  mistflowers, 174
  native plant gardens, 72
  snakes, 141
  and sustainable gardening, 97
  turtles, 117
  wildflowers, 52
Lady Bird Lake, *xxii*, 4, 13, 118
Lake Austin, 13, 103
landscaping, 65, 65–66, *66*, *67*, 78
Largeflower Crested Coralroot (*Hexalectris grandiflora*), 95

 *Index* 225